Business Issues, Competition and Entrepreneurship

AF848926

nova
science publishers
New York

Business Issues, Competition and Entrepreneurship

Performance Management for the Modern Leader
Verl Anderson, PhD (Author)
Cam Caldwell, PhD (Author)
2021. ISBN: 978-1-68507-336-7 (Hardcover)
2021. ISBN: 978-1-68507-415-9 (eBook)

Public-Private Partnerships: Trends, Perspectives and Opportunities
Diego Monferrer Tirado, PhD (Editor)
Beatriz Irún Molina, PhD (Editor)
2021. ISBN: 978-1-68507-184-4 (Hardcover)
2021. ISBN: 978-1-68507-292-6 (eBook)

Consumer Protection During the Pandemic
Georgina Conway (Author)
2021. ISBN: 978-1-68507-314-5 (Hardcover)
2021. ISBN: 978-1-68507-352-7 (eBook)

Risk Management: An Overview
Delfina Gabriela Garrido Ramos, PhD (Editor)
Luis Almeida (Editor)
2021. ISBN: 978-1-68507-177-6 (Hardcover)
2021. ISBN: 978-1-68507-242-1 (eBook)

Comprehending the Cognitive and Socio-Cultural Factors Affecting Entrepreneurship Intentions of Women in India: A GEM Data Based Approach
Bhavisha P. Sheth, PhD (Author)
Amit Kumar Dwivedi, PhD (Author)
2021. ISBN: 978-1-53619-633-7 (eBook)

More information about this series can be found at
https://novapublishers.com/product-category/series/business-issues-competition-and-entrepreneurship/

Arshi Naim
and
Praveen K. Malik
Editors

Competitive Trends and Technologies in Business Management

nova
science publishers
New York

https://doi.org/10.52305/VIXO9830

Library of Congress Cataloging-in-Publication Data

ISBN: 978-1-68507-612-2

Published by Nova Science Publishers, Inc. † New York

Contents

Preface

Competitive Trends and Technologies in Business Management clearly explains the global business management domain in the current scenario and covers the latest concepts in business and technologies for their successful implementation. The growth of global corporations has led to the development of new business strategies by the applications of new technologies. The critical success factors of business management depend on the successful applications of information systems and information technologies. To achieve competitive advantages, businesses are applying strategies from technological perspectives for various concepts such as customer relationship management, cost management, marketing management, etc. *Competitive Trends and Technologies in Business Management* describes the applications and concepts of IS in business management and presents the success stories of businesses. The book assesses competitive business management from an IS and IT perspective, examining business development policies linked to the profitability of global firms. The book covers comprehensive topics such as use of green technology in business processes, machine learning in business education, and artificial intelligence in the business sector. This book will drive readers to actively think through the most fundamental business concepts developed by IS and IT in the current competitive landscape and provides answers to questions such as: What are the new drivers of business management? and how do businesses apply IS and IT? The current Covid pandemic has caused serious financial loss to developing countries, and this book will help to explore new options of expanding markets for businesses by the applications of IS and IT.

Chapter 1 is "Applications of Decision Support Systems in CRM." This is an extended chapter where authors have built a model of Decision Support Systems (DSS) for facilitating the process of measuring profit and achieving customer satisfaction; also, the chapter shows the role of DSS in other fields of Marketing Management (M.Mgnt) and applications of DSS that can aid firms to meet their targets in sales and building relationships. The results show the positive impact of WIA and prove that this analytical method can be used by any customer-oriented firm as a general model for achieving positive outcomes.

***Chapter** 2*, "Successful E-CRM by the Application of Management Information Systems," presents the applications of Electronic Customer Relationship Management (CRM) for achieving customer satisfaction. The research chapter explains the theoretical concepts of MIS and E-CRM, shows how firms achieved major benefits by the applications of MIS, and shows how customer satisfaction was achieved by integrating MIS and E-CRM. The results show the variation and gaps in the application of MIS in E-CRM for the firm and after the applications. The annual report shows drastic growth, innovation and increase in customer satisfaction for the firm after the application of MIS in E-CRM.

***Chapter** 3* is "Applications of Green Information Technologies in Business Process Management." Green computing, also called Green Information Technologies (GIT), is the practice and procedures of using computing and other technological resources in a responsible and environmentally friendly manner. Climatic changes have raised concerns worldwide and countries are conducting summits to solve and prevent global warming. Information Technologies have been playing a great role in keeping the objectives of preserving the environment and one of the techniques is to apply green computing. The focus of GIT is to decrease the use of hazardous materials, reduce usage of energy, increase profit maximization and create awareness of the advantages of recyclability or biodegradability of computer trash. This paper presents the theoretical background of GIT and its roles and advantages for preserving climate. Also, this paper presents qualitative analysis on advantages and challenges of using GIT in business operations (BPO). These advantages are presented through very short instances and cases for the applications of GIT in BPO. GIT includes new services and products with optimum efficiency and possible options towards energy saving, so it provides the best way to keep the environment clean and healthy without trading off the use of technologies.

***Chapter** 4*, "Consumer Behavior appraisal for Health and Fitness Service", explains the psychographic aspect of consumer behavior for health services and efforts to understand how proactive behavior can be inculcated amongst consumers. Data was collected from primary sources, including medical practitioners, medical representatives and patients. Research method is adaptive as it tries to influence present psychographic consumer behavior towards health and fitness, and to measure responses, likert scale is used. To ensure optimal health and financial outcomes, the research method is both qualitative and quantitative. Structured and unstructured questionnaires are used for all primary sources, and for measuring some responses, tabulations are graphed for conclusive and descriptive findings. Consumers confidently choose products that provide the best value for the money. When it comes to choosing medicine and care, they often find themselves confused. Consumer organizations such as Consumers Union and Medical Organization can design programs or medical aid campaigns to help consumers select options that will provide optimal health and financial outcomes to fitness and health care so that consumers can have information about medical care as well as financial solutions to acquire fitness and health care. This research has contributed in two ways, firstly to know consumer behavior for health services for medical service providers so that they can develop communication programs, and secondly consumer awareness regarding medical care and financial aid.

Chapter 5 is "Economies of Scale for Security Applications in Business." This is an extended chapter, focusing on the economies of scale for organizations dealing with the crucial issues of security systems in business operations. Economies of scale are achieved by managing the cost. Information Technology (IT) is an important and irreplaceable need of society and all working sector's success depends on IT to a great extent; therefore, maintaining security features is one of the most important aspects of IT. When security is discussed in any business sector, Patch Management (P.Mgnt) has to be taken under account and is described in detail. P.Mgnt includes many concerns and areas to be described for IT security in business such as methods and problems in updating patch, methods of reducing security risks with P.Mgnt, methods of achieving economies of scale by controlling the operational costs and making decisions in investing when necessary. This chapter presents a general definition of Patch management, its benefits and management of working cost through theoretical models. Also, the chapter gives methods of feeding techniques for microstrip patch antenna MPA, showing the contracting and non-contracting methods.

Chapter 6 is "Virtual Learning in Business Information Systems: A Case Study on Quality Matters Applications." This is extended research work presenting the applications of broad multidimensional reference model of Quality Matters for E-Learning standards for blended courses and full online courses in such a way that learning outcomes of the module could be met. In this research paper, the importance and tasks of Quality Matters for course development and its relationship with E-Learning were defined and analyzed in the learning environment with special reference to Public University (PU) in Gulf for undergraduate students in Business Management curricula. This study clearly defined that the Reference Model of Quality Matters for E-Learning standards could be applied for all types of Modules such as Supportive, Blended or Full Online in learning paradigm that aids in meeting learning outcomes of business courses. Also, this study magnified the patterns of how QM standards facilitated E-Learning. The reference model of Quality Matters can be applied for all types of modules and programs.

Chapter 7 is "Application of Data Management System in Business-to-Business Electronic Commerce." E-commerce (EC) is a popular term, also occasionally known as Internet Commerce, which has grown drastically in the past few decades. Covid-19 has made most firms to consider EC as a necessity. EC has started to grow and Business to Business Electronic Commerce (B2BEC) too has been implemented by many businesses. The process includes the transaction of goods and services, the transfer of funds and the exchange of data virtually. B2BEC opens up new possibilities of trade and new business partners from around the globe can be found, their offers can be compared, complex negotiations can be conducted electronically, and a contract can be drawn up and fulfilled via an electronic marketplace. However, sophisticated data management is required to provide such facilities. On the other hand, the contribution of the researchers cannot be ignored in the present context, as they bring to light many pertinent issues and potential solutions with regards to the daily problems faced by society. The researchers are also responsible for unearthing issues that might become a point of concern in future. The researchers' work needs to be reviewed in a systematic way so as to identify the gaps where future research can be conducted and gaps can be filled. As database management has increasing relevance in the arena of B2BEC, it is crucial to check the holistic retrospective in this study in light of the literature available. As there is no review chapter till date in the arena of database management in B2BEC, the present chapter is dedicated to look for the same and propose gaps identified. For this purpose, the chapter adopts bibliometric analysis of SCOPUS database, i.e., the largest database for scientific studies.

Chapter 8 is "Applications of E-Learning tools for Achieving Students Learning Outcomes for Business program." This is the extended research presenting how applications of E-Learning tools aided in meeting students' learning outcomes and how students with different understanding and cognitive skills can get benefits from E-Learning tools. In the current research, researchers have tried to find the effectiveness of electronic tools for diverse skills. This research confers suggestions on how electronic tools in learning management services could be implemented by the instructors in the process of Learning and Teaching (LT) to meet the requirements of different learners in Information Systems (IS). In this study, the module chosen was Business Information Systems in Information System's environment. Thurstone scale to measure the effectiveness of various electronic tools is available on Learning Management Services (LMS) "Blackboard." This paper compared these electronic tools for their effectiveness in meeting learning outcomes for different learners in IS. For measuring assessments' results, three tools were used, namely Electronic-Quiz (EQ), Discussion Forum (DF) and Safe Assignment (SA). The paper has tried to measure the effectiveness of a new tool introduced on Blackboard named Safe Assignment for submitting assignments. Through this tool, instructors were able to identify the percentage of plagiarism or matching between the peers. Based on three assessments' results, namely EQ, DF and SA, samples were categorized under best, average and poor. These assessments were considered for the purpose of study because they were conducted by the implementation on electronic tool LMS. The performance of students in each group was analyzed and it was found that students in all groups could contribute and learn the best through open DF. Best Students tried to learn equally through all tools but the other two groups plant least efforts and submitted their assignments using search engines such as Google.

Chapter 9 is "Emerging Technologies in Finance and Market: Applications of AI." This is an extended chapter based on qualitative methods for the benefits of Artificial Intelligence (AI) which is the most growing branch of computer science and most of the service sectors are obtaining benefits from its application. This chapter provides a general role of AI in financial services and its definition in practical scenarios. The study is mostly qualitative and does not include any data analysis for its results. This article describes the major benefits derived by the practices of AI in general in the banking and financing firms. For the study, some examples of the role of AI in financial firms are analyzed and results are given from the positive observation shared by the FI firms on their official website. Since the data are available publically, the chapter did not find issues of data privacy and gave all references of data sources. AI benefits both service providers and users; this research report explains the advantages of AI in finance and also describes how AI can aid in market development. This chapter contributes positively in understanding the relevance of AI, particularly in the field of finance.

Acknowledgments

First of all, we would like to thank the Almighty Lord for giving us the opportunity and guidance to achieve our goal and to be successful in this part. We would like to thank our family for their tireless efforts and support in every path. Last but not least, we would also like to thank the publisher, editors, and support staff at Nova Science Publishers, as they were very helpful in the various stages of developing and producing the volume.

Dr. Arshi Naim
Dr. Praveen Kumar Malik

Chapter 1

Applications of Decision Support Systems in CRM

Arshi Naim* and Kholood Alqahtani†
Department of Information Systems, King Khalid University,
Abha, Kingdom of Saudi Arabia (KSA)

Abstract

This is an extended chapter where we have built a model of Decision Support Systems (DSS) for facilitating the process of measuring profit and achieving customer satisfaction also the chapter shows the role of DSS in other fields of Marketing Management (M.Mgnt) and applications of DSS that can aid the firms to meet their target in sales and building relationships. DSS facilitates in decision making process for many M.Mgnt concepts and Customer Relationship Management (CRM) is one of them and it depends on the firm's tasks for developing and retaining customers while achieving their satisfaction and enhancing the sense of belongingness for their products and services. Profit maximization, the process of customer value, and building strategic values for the firm are the three empirical benefits of CRM that are achieved through analytical, operational, and direction (AOD) capabilities respectively. This research focuses on the application of DSS models of what-if analysis (WIA) for CRM at (AOD) and also shows the dependence on the Information Success model (ISM). This is a review chapter presenting the comparative analysis between two firms in fast

* Corresponding Author's Email: arshi@kku.edu.sa.
† Corresponding Author's Email: kaljbar@kku.edu.sa.

In: Competitive Trends and Technologies in Business Management
Editors: Arshi Naim and Praveen K. Malik
ISBN: 978-1-68507-612-2

moving consumer goods (FMCG) where one applied WIA for all three levels and one did not apply. Firms' data are analyzed for (AOD) by three types of (WIA) to attain CRM and profit maximization. The results show positive impact of WIA and prove that this analytical method can be used by any customer-oriented firm as a general model for achieving positive outcomes.

Keywords: information success model, CRM, DSS, analytical, operational, directional, what if analysis

1. Introduction

IS application is a collection of interrelated elements that work collaboratively to convert data into information that is used to support various organizational activities including control, planning, forecasting, decision making, coordination, and operational activities [4, 5] and DSS is one of its important application that helps in the above tasks. DSS can help organization's employees and managers in visualizing complex subjects, create new products, and problems analysis. Nowadays IS applications in the business area can be categorized into different types such as support of business operations or support of managerial decision making [6]. Any ideal organization applies six major applications of IS such as Transaction Processing System (TPS), Office Automation System (OAS), Knowledge Work System (KWS), Management Information System (MIS), Executive Support System (ESS), Decision Support System (DSS) [7, 8, 9]. Figure 1 shows the types and basic information about the IS applications.

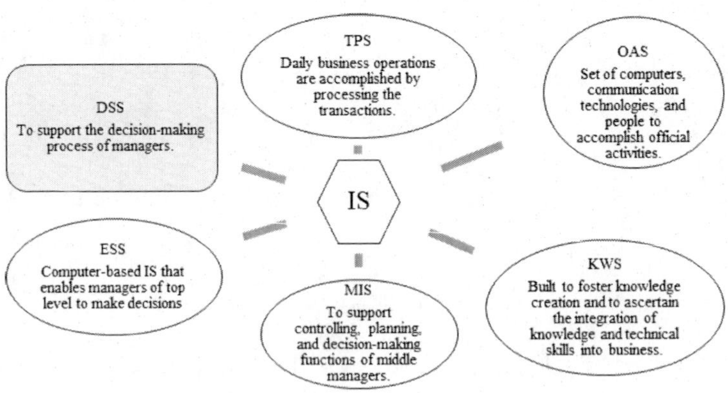

Figure 1. Types of IS Applications [9].

Customer relationship management (CRM) [1] is the branch of management that gives the scope of operational demonstration of relationship marketing and explains the characteristics of a customer, criterion and features for developing relationship between customers and firms, achieving customer loyalty and way of customers' retention, firms, therefore, apply CRM to explore prospects for their products and services, understand customer's requirements and their expectation for quality [1, 2]. CRM is particularly regarded as the firm's efforts to develop and retain customers through increased satisfaction and loyalty. DSS-based CRM systems have been applied in many business areas, and R&D is continuing to contribute to its expansion [3].

DSS works for four phases of decision making process such as Intelligence, Design, Choose and Implementations (IDCI) and for all these phases application of DSS works in problem solving. This application is WIA which has three tools described earlier in this chapter; contributes in finding the solutions for each phase. These tools are SBWIA, GSWIA and DBWIA.

Table 1. DSS (WIA) supporting the decisions [12]

DSS		
WIA		
Phases	**Tools**	**Management Discipline**
IDCI	SBWIA/GSWIA/DBWIA	CRM/SCM/Expert System

This research is based on the application of (WIA) which is the DSS model-based analysis for three levels of (AOD) of CRM. DSS (WIA) is a computer-based application aiding in the decision making process for management related areas such as SCM, ERP, CRM, etc. (WIA) aids CRM in managing customers' inquiries and also in attracting, retaining, developing, and identifying customers and figure 2 gives a framework of DSS (WIA) for how decisions are supported for different management decisions [9, 10].

This research paper is segmented into six parts; the first part gives an introduction and the second part covers the historical aspects of concepts used in this paper and previous studies showing the contribution of DSS (WIA) in management in general and specifically in CRM. The third part gives the details on conceptual hypothesis and Research methodology, the fourth part covers the major explanation of the research procedure and implications in Discussion. In the fifth and sixth part results and findings are illustrated followed by a conclusion. This research paper shows the application of DSS (WIA) in customer-oriented firms at three levels (AOD) for achieving profit and building relationships and eventually impacting CRM by the use of hypothetical data.

2. Literature Review

Before the 1960s, the IS role was simple, basically, was used to achieve the goals of electronic data processing (EDP), such as accounting and transaction processing. EDP is defined as the use of a computer to perform various processes on data including summarizing, classifying, manipulating, and recording. EDP is also called transaction processing systems (TPS) [10, 14].

In the 1960s, other functions were added to IS which were for processing of data into useful informative reports, and MIS was therefore introduced. MIS gave new roles to the managers, they started to use IS for making decisions and developing business applications with the IS contribution [10, 14].

By the 1970s, the IS reports produced by MIS were not enough to satisfy the management decision-making needs that were when (DSS) emerged and it provided computer-based interaction and specialized support for managers and end-users to facilitate decision-making processes [11, 15]. End users now could support their job requirements by using their own computing resources; they did not need to wait for a centralized corporate information services department to provide indirect support. In later years EIS [13] and AI were techniques introduced with different advantages and scope. ES and KMS gave a new role to IS in the late 90s and 1990 ERP emerged for corporate resource planning and allocation [13, 15]. In the same era, internet growth started that gave a new significance to all the IS applications and DSS applications became very popular in the decision making process in management systems particularly for CRM [10, 14, 16].

Past researches have shown how firm's use CRM for motivating their employees to essentially develop customer-focused thinking [16] and here IS has played an important role as a technology solution. In the past, researchers have focused on methods of IS affecting customer-oriented firms for CRM profitability and also formulated models such as the CRM profitability model from relationship marketing and system efficiency perspective [15, 16, 17].

Previous studies have shown the importance of using software applications and technology for different types of management disciplines such as SCM, ERP, or CRM, but the expected results for CRM are not achieved because of its qualitative nature. However, CRM continued to apply IS applications for various purposes and identified different impact factors of

IS applications for different levels of CRM but DSS is one application found to be most effective working for the achievement of CRM objectives [15, 16, 17]. Previous studies have shown the relationship of DSS for CRM but this research paper gives an analysis of the application of DSS (WIA) for showing the results for CRM at all three levels and suggests the same model for any customer-oriented firms for their applications [18].

Research also presents the dependence of ISM with CRM for building brand image, increasing sales, strategic planning but this research paper also covers the aspects of ISM for CRM and how both can be considered for providing the research findings.

3. Theoretical Perspectives of Research Methodology

CRM provides its services to firms at three levels; Analytical, Operational, and Directional levels (AOD), and each level benefits the firm in some way that eventually contributes to achieving CRM. (WIA) facilitates in building these levels and offers decision-making solutions to structured, semi-structured, and unstructured decisions for these levels. Figure 3 depicts the research framework used for this chapter.

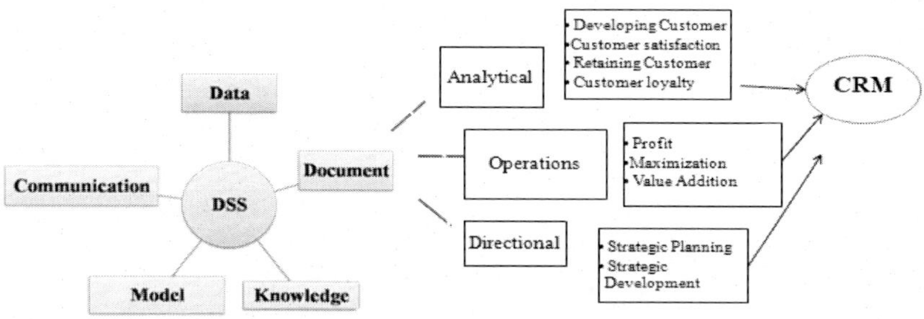

Figure 3. Research Framework: Role of WIA in CRM [18].

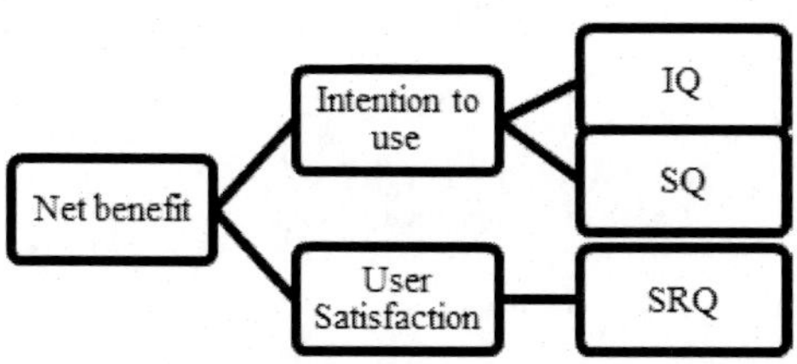

Figure 4. ISM by Delone and McLean [19].

The results are presented by retrieving data from two FMCG firms, DSS decision-making models are applied to these three examples for all three CRM's levels and results are analyzed from (WIA) applications. The results are measured for three levels (AOD) by (WIA) and show its impact on CRM. To understand how the information from these three examples can be helpful for CRM, Delone, and McLean's perspective of ISM can be referred [19]. The ISM has been treated as a major issue of management research for any type of service for measuring satisfaction. DeLone and McLean have taken six major categories of measures of IS application like DSS success which are seen to form an integrated whole [19]. These measures are System Quality (SQ), Information Quality (IQ), Service Quality (SRQ), resulting to use and user satisfaction and finally to individual impact, and organizational impact and all these measures are a subpart of three levels (AOD) of CRM [19]. IQ, SQ, and SRQ measure A, SQ, and SRQ measure O, and SRQ measure D. Figure 5 depict how ISM is used in our study for preparing the criteria for measuring AOD. These criteria are used as inputs for decision-making processes by (WIA) based such as Scenario-based, Goal seeking, and Data-based for CRM. These criteria and information are extracted from the hypothetical data for three examples submitted for different services for three months (from March to May 2020) and show how the target of CRM can be achieved in the next month June 2020 for all three AOD levels using a classification of Information Success model.

IQ, SQ, SRQ (A)

- A1:Developing Customer (DC)
- A2: Customer satisfaction (CS)
- A3: Retaining Customer (RC)
- A4: Customer loyalty (CL)

SQ, SRQ (O)

- O1:Profit Maximization (PM)
- O2: Value Addition (VA)

SRQ (D)

- D1 Strategic Planning (SP)
- D2: Strategic Development (SD)

Figure 5. Criteria for ISM for (AOD) [20].

CRM has scope in wide range of marketing practices therefore if the firm is able to achieve or implement CRM, as a result it may be able to achieve related areas of CRM such as marketing and brand image, providing customer services, customer loyalty, customer satisfaction, supply chain, sales, etc. It also explains that CRM success is the success of many other branches of marketing.

4. Discussion

Most of the service-oriented firms focus on achieving CRM by having customer interaction and creating an opportunity for increasing satisfaction level, improving retention, increasing revenue or profit, attain brand loyalty, strengthen brand value, etc. CRM helps service firms in particular and all other businesses, in general, to optimize customer relationships by integrating at the AOD level.

The CRM Advantages for customer-oriented firms: CRM reduces the time and cost to deploy integrated advantages with a comprehensive set of solutions based on the principles of services and types of levels. These benefits help inefficient business operations, receiving updated and accurate information, vision for successful business applications [23].

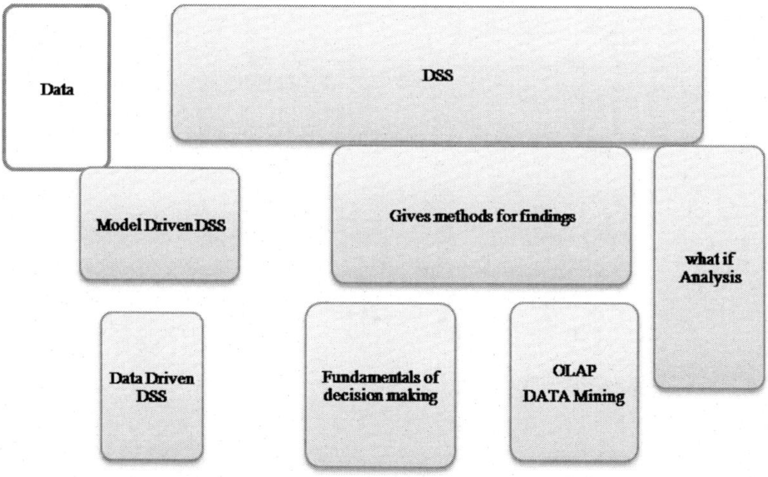

Figure 6. Types of DSS [25, 26].

(WIA) provides computer-aided decision-making solutions to CRM for (AOD) and helps in getting the key benefits such as identifying customers' preferences, integrating management services, increase productivity, achieving CS and CR, building brand image and brand loyalty, increase sales. All these benefits can be received by the CRM with an application of (WIA).

DSS works for user by the application of WIA and this application uses its three tools for building user interface and finally provides benefit to the user. DSS (WIA) offers the advantages to CRM and that results in many benefits to the firm in general such as achieving competitive advantages, identifying business opportunities, receiving quick customers' responses, increasing sales, knowing demand value and customers' expectations. Figure 7 shows the framework of DSS (WIA) that can be applied for user interfaces for receiving users' reviews and expectations by its three types. Types of Decision-Support Systems: There are major two types of DSS, data-based, and model-based. (WIA) are a model-based DSS and below given Figure 6 shows the basic types of DSS [20, 21, 22].

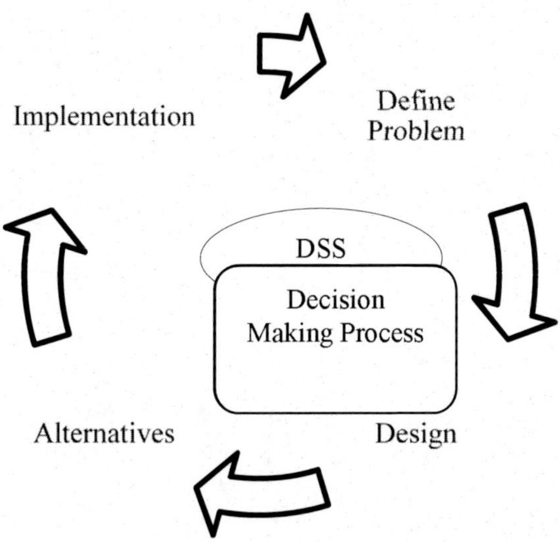

Figure 7. Framework of DSS Decision Making Process [26].

5. Research Procedure

General scenario: Three sets of criteria are developed for each level as mentioned in Figure 5, referring to these criteria, two FMCG's data are taken as examples and studied in the framework of DSS to find out how DSS (WIA) can facilitate the decision-making process from structure to unstructured for each CRM. It is important to notice that (WIA) makes only recommendations not the results in absolute terms; it facilitates the decision-making process but does not force to implementation of a particular scenario. As mentioned above there are three types of (WIA); Scenario based (SBWIA), Goal Seeking (GSWIA), and Data-Based (DBWIA), for the three levels of CRM aligned with Information success models, all three types of (WIA) can be implemented for showing its impact on CRM. Below given tables below show the three Examples for three levels (AOD) aligned for the information success model, criteria used by three different types of (WIA). Example-1 shows the analytical scenario for the month's March, April, and May for A1: Developing customer (DC), A2: Customer Satisfaction (CS), A3: Retaining Customer (RC), A4: Customer Loyalty (CL) and the firm strives for higher growth for each criterion for the month of June. The firm can use SBWIA and while elaborating the target for each criterion and set a scenario to achieve that. To show the results we compare two firms, one applying WIA and one without applying WIA for all three levels such as (AOD) and for the accuracy of the application both FMCG firms are accounted for the same targets and other values.

Table 2. Analytical by SBWIA

IQ,SQ,SRQ (A) [Analyzed by SBWIA					**Not Applied SBWIA**			
Criteria	**FMCG1**				**FMCG2**			
	March	**April**	**May**	**June [Target]**	**March**	**April**	**May**	**June [Target]**
A1:DC	4000	5000	5500	8000	4000	5000	5500	8000
A2: CS	4000	5000	6000	8000	4000	5000	6000	8000
A3:RC	4000	5000	5500	8000	4000	5000	5500	8000
A4: CL	4000	5000	5500	8000	4000	5000	5500	8000

FMCG1 and FMCG 2 both target to achieve 8000 sales in the month of June, researchers have discussed this in results if FMCG 2 was able to achieve its target in the month of June without applying SBWIA for all criteria.

Table 3 depicts the profit for the example-2 for three months and by using DBWIA, the firm can predict O1 and O2 for the month of June and coming months. These figures are shown in sales and DBWIA helps in manipulating data for achieving the target sales. Example-2 also shows the variation as an increase and decrease in profit and value addition that usually occur in real situations so how DBWIA facilitated in predicting the Operational level CRM for all the criteria O1: Profit Maximization (PM) and O2: Value Addition (VA). In this situation FMCG 1 and FMCG 2 are compared and the results show that FMCG1 was able to predict the results for risk management whereas FMCG was not able to predict accurately. It is important to mention that DBWIA at the operational level only provides values for prediction but possible decision-making analysis has to be conducted through SBWIA or GSWIA.

Table 3. Operation by DBWIA

ISQ,SRQ (O) [Analyzed by DBWIA					**Not Applied DBWIA**			
Criteria	**FMCG1**				**FMCG2**			
	March	**April**	**May**	**June[Target]**	**March**	**April**	**May**	**June[Target]**
O1: PM	5000	6000	5500	8000	5000	6000	5500	8000
O2: VA	5000	4500	6000	8000	5000	4500	6000	8000

Table 4 shows the directional level in CRM explains the strategic achievement for the products, services, and policies of the form in general. Usually, Directional level CRM focuses on short to long-term achievements, below given table shows two criteria such as D1: Strategic Planning (SP) and D2: Strategic Development (SD) at Directional level CRM and measured by GSWIA. Goals are set for 2020-23 and analyzed from 2010-13 for criteria D1 and D2. Usually, data set for this level can be extracted from sales inferred through brand effectiveness or brand image.

Table 4. Directional by GBWIA

SRQ (D) [Analyzed by GSWIA					**Not Applied GSWIA**			
Criteria	**FMCG1**				**FMCG2**			
	2010-13	**2013-16**	**2016-19**	**2020-23**	**2010-13**	**2013-16**	**2016-19**	**2020-23**
D1: SP	4000	5000	5500	8000	4000	5000	5500	8000
D2: SD	4000	5000	6000	8000	4000	5000	6000	8000

Data collected from these examples are analyzed by (WIA) for decision making for achieving CRM for all these three levels and recommendations are made in the results section. (WIA) suggests which area is weak and the firm's need to concentrate on changing their strategies for meeting their goals. In above given three examples (WIA) stresses the prompt changes with minimum efforts and also provides assumptions for future improvements and meeting the target for the month of June for all three levels for CRM. (WIA) is applied at three levels and presents how targets can be met by supporting strongly the tools of decision-making processes. From the above given three examples in Tables 2, 3, and 4 customer-oriented firms can refer (WIA) for AOD and can achieve the following benefits specified as criteria for AOD in CRM and ISM. Below given Table 5 gives a comprehensive view and derived benefits from interrelationships between CRM, ISM, AOD, and (WIA) but details on findings from above mentioned data for FMCG1 and 2 in three examples are discussed in the results' part and Table 6 explains all benefits in detail aligned criteria of AOD in the result section.

Table 5. Derived benefits from (WIA) models for AOD

CRM levels and ISM	**DSS models based on WIA**	**Advantages**
IQ, SQ, SRQ (A)		
A1: DC	Analyzed by SBWIA	Customer Orientation (CO)
A2: CS		Information Quality Perception (IQP)
A3: RC		Value Addition in Services (VAS)
A4:CL		Supporting Customers and grievance handing (SCGH)
SQ, SRQ (O)		
O1: PM	Analyzed by DBWIA	Achieving Profit through Sales (PS)
O2: VA		VAS
SRQ (D)		
D1: SP	Analyzed by GSWIA	Enhancing Brand value (BV) and increase systems efficiency (SE)
D2: SD		Performance based policies (PBP) for long run and System Support (SSP)

5. Results

The study covers the application of (WIA) for CRM for three levels of AOD using ISM. This study is based on a hypothetical data set that tried to explain how the DSS model-based can help in CRM for AOD.

CRM (CO): CO refers to the commitment of the firm to identify and satisfy customer concerns and develop more customers through providing quality services. SBWIA gives the situation like quality for longer period of time and meet demand for new services about the quality and measures if more customers are developed for the particular services or not. SBWIA also explains how the given target can be met through elaborating the contingent approach. Results sections shows how A1 grows by using DSS model based SBWIA.

CRM (IQP): SBWIA facilitates at a level of CRM to measure if customers are satisfied or not for that SBWIA creates a scenario for customers related to quality, reliability of information and after sales services as well then make a target for achieving it after implementation of this scenario. SBWIA takes the data from the previous month to show the variations to meet the target.

CRM (VAS): Customer retention is the results of customer satisfaction which can be achieved through values added services, technology has played a great role in adding values and increasing retention rate, SBWIA creates a scenario for the past data for customer retention rate and based on that gives the variation from the expected retention target. Results provide clear understanding through scenario analysis for the data for shown in Table 3. CRM (VAS) is also a benefit for level O2 which measures the values addition in quantitative terms and it is measured by DBWIA.

CRM (SCGH): To achieve customer loyalty, there are many factors to be considered by CRM; therefore scenario for A4 needs to refer many dimensions such as providing services of good quality on time, listening to the customer complaints, their reactions and eventually attaining customers' loyalty. There are some philosophies that give a direct relation between customer reactions to customer loyalty in relation to CRM performance for identifying the scenario for A4, SBWIA considers many few situations such as reaction to overall results of the customer's awareness, appraisal, and psychological feedback to the utilization experience with the product or service. As customer loyalty is commonly acknowledged as one of the most useful measurements of level A of CRM as it measures profitability, satisfaction and retention. Results for Table 1 shows for A4 and how it achieves its target while comparing from past data to expected data for the scenario created.

CRM (PS): At the operational level of CRM and from an ISM perspective, business process improvement that assures efficiency and excellence of enterprise operations is an important to be measured, therefore DBWIA is used to analyze previous months' sales and revenue and based on past trends predict the future sales and revenue for the firms. In this analysis CRM needs DSS model based approach for marketing, sales and earning maximum profits for the firm.

CRM (SE): ISM and CRM work together at D level to build strategic planning for the firm where the major focus is brand loyalty, building brand image and strengthening the brand therefore GSWIA is the best DSS model to be implemented which sets the target and then make a plan for achieving it. GBWIA helps in decision making process and make possible recommendations for variations. Example-3 shows how data at D1 levels are aided by GSWIA for the successful of strategic planning. This process included many predetermined goals, parameters such as cost, time, function and efficiency in which they should be achieved. The assumption on which GSWIA works for D1 is that the relationships between CRM efficiency and customer reaction are managed by all CRM activities like customer reaction, perception, loyalty, retention and all contribute in strategic planning.

CRM (SSP): D2 level of CRM is measured by GSWIA by measuring the performance of the firms based on what strategies were developed to attain that level. Also GSWIA studies the previous data for D2 and identifies that successful strategies bring more profits to the firm and contribute in customer satisfaction. Firms use GSWIA to measure of the D2 CRM for systems' performance and assume if the system has been implemented and adopted successfully all criteria such as resource utilization; reliability, response time, and ease of terminal use; data accuracy, reliability, completeness, system flexibility, and ease of use; consistency of the user interface, quality of documentation, and sometimes, quality and maintainability be able to reap its benefits.

The results show the high degree of relevance and dependence on (WIA) for three examples. Example in Table 6 shows the role of SBWIA in successfully predicting the values for the month of June at an analytical level for four criteria which are developing customers, achieving satisfaction, retention, and loyalty.

Table 6. SBWIA for level A of CRM

IQ,SQ,SRQ (A) [Analyzed by SBWIA					**Not Applied SBWIA**			
Criteria	**FMCG1**				**FMCG2**			
	March	**April**	**May**	**June [Results]**	**March**	**April**	**May**	**June [Result]**
A1:DC	4000	5000	5500	8000	4000	5000	5500	6000
A2: CS	4000	5000	6000	8000	4000	5000	6000	6500
A3:RC	4000	5000	5500	8000	4000	5000	5500	6000
A4: CL	4000	5000	5500	8000	4000	5000	5500	6000

Highlighted cells show the successful application of SBWIA for A1, A2, A3, and A4 but FMCG 2 which did not apply the SBWIA show the normal trend of growth and were unable to achieve the target. Table 3 focuses on operational benefits of CRM that are expressed in sale and revenue therefore DBWIA is here and Table 8 shows the variation in target and how DBWIA can help firms to know the areas where they need to work to achieve the target value that will result in achieving level O of CRM. The results show the variation for each month against the target value required to be achieved in the month of June, therefore after applying DBWIA firms can get the variation at each level and needed values too for meeting the target as shown in Table 8. Also the results in the Table 8 the presents the comparison between two firms where FMCG2 could not accurately predict the trend and was not able to hit the target.

The results clearly show that the FMCG1 was able to calculate the variation by the application of DBWIA needed for O1 and O2 for the month June to achieve the target and FMCG2 could not predict the variation and therefore was unable to meet the target. Application of DBWIA is an easy and simple process and firms of all nature extensively apply in achieving PM and creating VA.

Table 7. DBWIA for level O

ISQ,SRQ (O) [Analyzed by DBWIA					**Not Applied DBWIA**			
Criteria	**FMCG1**				**FMCG2**			
	March	**April**	**May**	**June [Target]**	**March**	**April**	**May**	**June [Target]**
O1: PM	5000	6000	5500	8000	5000	6000	5500	8000
O2: VA	5000	4500	6000	8000	5000	4500	6000	8000
ISQ,SRQ (O) [Analyzed by DBWIA					Not Applied DBWIA			
Criteria	Variation to the target Applied							
	March	April	May	DBWIA Applied	March	April	May	DBWIA not Applied
O1: PM	3000	2000	2500	8000	2000	1500	2500	7000
O2: VA	3000	3500	2000	8000	2000	1500	2000	6000

Table 8. GSWIA for level D

SRQ (D) [Analyzed by GSWIA							**Not Applied GSWIA**			
Criteria	**FMCG1**						**FMCG2**			
	2010-13	**2013-16**	**2016-19**	**2020-23**			**2010-13**	**2013-16**	**2016-19**	**2020-23**
D1: SP	4000	5000	5500	8000			4000	5000	5500	8000
D2: SD	4000	5000	6000	8000			4000	5000	6000	8000
SRQ (D) [Analyzed by GSWIA							Not Applied GSWIA			
Criteria	FMCG1						FMCG2			
	2010-13	2013-16	2016-19	Average Variation	Missing target to Achieve	2020-13 [T]	2010-13	2013-16	2016-19	2020-23
D1: SP	4000	5000	5500	4833.333	-3355	8000	4000	5000	5500	6000
D2: SD	4000	5000	6000	5000	3355	8000	4000	5000	6000	6000

Table 8, shows the results on long term planning for both the firms, one applied GSWIA and second firm did not apply rather based on past trend tried to achieve the SP and SD.

The results clearly show that tools of WIA work not only immediate results but also for long term planning. FMCG 1 applied GSWIA for its two levels D1 and D2 was able to identify the variation and requirement for meeting the target in the coming years, whereas FMCG 2 continued the process of SP and SD without the application of GSWIA and was unable to achieve its objectives in the long run.

Conclusion

In the current scenario it is observed that IS has facilitated all the disciplines and marketing management and its related fields are widely benefitted by its applications. Out of all applications of IS, DSS is the most popular one because it it able to facilitate the firms in decision making process for structured and unstructured problems. The DSS has some tools and tools of WIA are applied in this research paper to show the success model of firms using the WIA in comparison to the firm not using the WIA.

CRM is one of the most important areas in management and DSS (WIA) is one of the relevant methods for the decision-making process. This research presents a general scenario through a comparative analysis and it can be applied for any customer-oriented firm for using (WIA) impacting CRM where this model facilitates in developing CS, CR, CL and also to contribute in sales and revenue along with the measuring the effectiveness of strategic planning for future growth. The research expects the major growth of IS and specifically DSS in more disciplines for the CRM, PM, VA and over all development.

References

[1] Raab, G., Ajami, R. A., & Goddard, G. J. (2016). *Customer relationship management: A global perspective.* CRC Press.

[2] Peppers, D., & Rogers, M. (2004). *Managing customer relationships: A strategic framework.* John Wiley & Sons.

[3] Chan, S. L., & Ip, W. H. (2011). A dynamic decision support system to predict the value of customer for new product development. *Decision support systems,* 52(1), 178-188.

[4] Grover, V., Chiang, R. H., Liang, T. P., & Zhang, D. (2018). Creating strategic business value from big data analytics: A research framework. *Journal of Management Information Systems,* 35(2), 388-423.

[5] Filip, F. G. (2020). DSS—A Class of Evolving Information Systems. In *Data Science: New Issues, Challenges and Applications* (pp. 253-277). Springer, Cham.

[6] Naim, A. (2018). Strategies to Achieve Students' Centric Approach in Blended Learning. *International Journal of Engineering and Management Research (IJEMR),* 8(2), 214-219.

[7] Appelbaum, D., Kogan, A., Vasarhelyi, M., & Yan, Z. (2017). Impact of business analytics and enterprise systems on managerial accounting. *International Journal of Accounting Information Systems,* 25, 29-44.

[8] Pavoine, S., Vallet, J., Dufour, A. B., Gachet, S., & Daniel, H. (2009). On the challenge of treating various types of variables: application for improving the measurement of functional diversity. Oikos, 118(3), 391-402.

[9] Kaiser, R., Spiegel, P. B., Henderson, A. K., & Gerber, M. L. (2003). The application of geographic information systems and global positioning systems in humanitarian emergencies: lessons learned, programme implications and future research. *Disasters,* 27(2), 127-140.

[10] Naim, A., Sattar, R. A., Al Ahmary, N.., & Razwi, M. T. (2021) Implementation of Quality Matters Standards on Blended Courses: A Case Study. *FINANCE INDIA Indian Institute of Finance* Vol. XXXV No. 3, September 2021 Pages—873–890.

[11] O'brien, J. A., & Marakas, G. M. (2005). *Introduction to information systems* (Vol. 13). New York City, USA: McGraw-Hill/Irwin.

[12] Arnott, D. (2004). Decision support systems evolution: framework, case study and research agenda. *European Journal of Information Systems,* 13(4), 247-259.

[13] Watson, H. J. (2018). Revisiting Ralph Sprague's framework for developing decision support systems. *Communications of the Association for Information Systems,* 42(1), 13.

[14] Aronson, J. E., Liang, T. P., & MacCarthy, R. V. (2005). *Decision support systems and intelligent systems* (Vol. 4). Upper Saddle River, NJ, USA. Pearson Prentice-Hall.

[15] Sharkey, U., & Acton, T. (2012). *Innovations in information systems from transaction processing to expert systems.*

[16] Polkowski, L., Tsumoto, S., & Lin, T. Y. (Eds.). (2012). *Rough set methods and applications: new developments in knowledge discovery in information systems* (Vol. 56). Physica.

[17] Naim, A. (2021). Application of Quality Matters in Digital Learning in Higher Education. *Texas Journal of Multidisciplinary Studies,* 1(1), 3-12.

[18] Jia, P., Cheng, X., Xue, H., & Wang, Y. (2017). Applications of geographic information systems (GIS) data and methods in obesity-related research. *Obesity reviews,* 18(4), 400-411.

[19] Sigala, M. (2018). Implementing social customer relationship management. *International Journal of Contemporary Hospitality Management.*

[20] Naim, A., & Bashir, A. (2016). Application of Quality Matters Standards on Supportive and Online Module in Higher Education Program. *Research Revolution,* 5(3), 6-12.

[21] Watanabe, C., & Hobo, M. (2004). Co-evolution between internal motivation and external expectation as a source of firm self-propagating function creation. *Technovation,* 24(2), 109-120.

[22] Hussain, M. R., Naim, A., & Khaleel, M. A. (2020). Implementation of Wireless Sensor Network Using Virtual Machine (VM) for Insect Monitoring. *Innovations in Electronics and Communication Engineering: Proceedings of the 8th ICIECE* 2019, 107, 73.

[23] Alt, R., & Puschmann, T. (2004, January). Successful practices in customer relationship management. In 37th Annual Hawaii International Conference on System Sciences, 2004. Proceedings of the (pp. 9-pp). IEEE.

[24] Naim, A., Khan, M. F., Hussain, M. R., & Khan, N. (2019). "Virtual Doctor" Management Technique in the Diagnosis of ENT Diseases. *JOE,* 15(9), 88.

[25] Delone, W. H., & McLean, E. R. (2003). The DeLone and McLean model of information systems success: a ten-year update. *Journal of management information systems,* 19(4), 9-30.

[26] Foss, B., Stone, M., & Ekinci, Y. (2008). What makes for CRM system success—Or failure?. *Journal of Database Marketing & Customer Strategy Management,* 15(2), 68-78.

[27] Naim, A., Alahmari, F., & Rahim, A. (2021). Role of Artificial Intelligence in Market Development and Vehicular Communication. *Smart Antennas: Recent Trends in Design and Applications,* 2, 28.

[28] Cuthbertson, R., & Laine, A. (2003). The role of CRM within retail loyalty marketing. *Journal of Targeting, Measurement and Analysis for Marketing,* 12(3), 290-304.

[29] Naim, A., & Alahmari, F. (2020). Reference model of e-learning and quality to establish interoperability in higher education systems. *International Journal of Emerging Technologies in Learning (iJET),* 15(2), 15-28.

[30] Collins, K. (2001). Analytical CRM: Driving Profitable Customer Relationships. Strategic Planning.

[31] Friday, D., Ryan, S., Sridharan, R., & Collins, D. (2018). Collaborative risk management: a systematic literature review. *International Journal of Physical Distribution & Logistics Management.*

[32] Hussain, M. R., Quadri, N. N., Ahmad, N., Qamar, S., Khan, N., Naim, A., & Hussain, M. E. (2019, April). Effective cost optimization approach in Healthcare to minimize the treatment cost of Brain-tumor Patients. In 2019 International Conference on Computer and Information Sciences (ICCIS) (pp. 1-5). IEEE.

[33] Eom, S. (2020, May). DSS, BI, and Data Analytics Research: Current State and Emerging Trends (2015–2019). In International Conference on Decision Support System Technology (pp. 167-179). Springer, Cham.

[34] Naim, A., Hussain, M. R., Naveed, Q. N., Ahmad, N., Qamar, S., Khan, N., & Hweij, T. A. (2019, April). Ensuring interoperability of e-learning and quality development in education. In 2019 IEEE Jordan International Joint Conference on Electrical Engineering and Information Technology (JEEIT) (pp. 736-741). IEEE.

[35] Rupnik, R., & Kukar, M. (2007). Decision support system to support decision processes with data mining. *Journal of information and organizational sciences,* 31(1), 217-232.

[36] Khan, N., Naim, A., Hussain, M. R., Naveed, Q. N., Ahmad, N., & Qamar, S. (2019, May). The 51 v's of big data: survey, technologies, characteristics, opportunities, issues and challenges. In Proceedings of the international conference on omni-layer intelligent systems (pp. 19-24).

[37] Asemi, A., Safari, A., & Zavareh, A. A. (2011). The role of management information system (MIS) and Decision support system (DSS) for manager's decision making process. *International Journal of Business and Management,* 6(7), 164-173.

Chapter 2

Successful E-CRM by the Application of Management Information Systems

Arshi Naim*
Department of Information Systems, King Khalid University,
Abha, Kingdom of Saudi Arabia (KSA)

Abstract

In the recent years Customer Relationship Management (CRM) has made significant step world over for effective aid to serve customers. During last two years pandemic is suffered globally due to novel virus COVID-19. In this situation Information systems (IS) and E-commerce witnessed not only major growth but also contributed to social and customer benefits. In this chapter, one of the important applications of IS, which is Management Information Systems (MIS) is applied for the purpose of achieving CRM electronically. Management Information Systems has strengthened CRM and firms who have enhanced their business through E-Commerce are known as E-CRM. This paper reviews and presents the developments in E-CRM through MIS with one of the examples from Dairy Corporation 'Almarai", working successfully in the region of KSA. The research paper explains the theoretical concepts of MIS and E-CRM and also shows through this example how the firm achieved major benefits by the applications of MIS and how customer satisfaction was achieved by integrating MIS and E-CRM. The results show the variation and gaps before the application of MIS in E-CRM for the firm and after the applications. The annual report shows drastic growth,

* Corresponding Author's Email: arshi@kku.edu.sa.

In: Competitive Trends and Technologies in Business Management
Editors: Arshi Naim and Praveen K. Malik
ISBN: 978-1-68507-612-2

innovation and increase in customer satisfaction for the firm after the application of MIS in E-CRM.

Keywords: customer relationship management, management information system, e-commerce, customer satisfaction

1. Introduction

In recent years CRM has made significant step world over as an effective aid to serve customers. Management Information Systems has strengthened CRM in all ways and firms who have enhanced their business online through E-Commerce, commonly known as E-CRM, it has consequence as a boom to success. Customer relationship marketing (CRM) is a business process in which client relationships, customer loyalty and brand value are built through marketing strategies and activities. CRM allows businesses to develop long-term relationships with established and new customers while helping streamline corporate performance. CRM incorporates commercial and client-specific strategies via employee training, marketing planning, relationship building and advertising [1].

CRM's core strength is an ability to glean insight from customer feedback to create enhanced, solid and focused marketing and brand awareness. Key motivating drivers for the development of more innovative CRM strategies are Web technologies and a sharpened global focus on customer loyalty. CRM also provides a way to directly evaluate customer value. For example, a business that is genuinely interested in its customers is rewarded with customer and brand loyalty. Because CRM is mutually advantageous, market share viability advances at a sound pace. E-Commerce provides cross-selling opportunities based on customer approval to businesses, this may pitch proven marketing or brand strategies to more than one clients or firms [1].

Customer relationship marketing should not be confused with "customer relationship management," it is related, but has unique concept and applications. Both share the same acronym which is CRM.

There may be hardly any organization which in some way or the other is not using CRM philosophy. As the companies make the transition from a product-only focus to a customer focus, CRM emerges as a technology that brings customers closer to organizations to retrieve online information. Customer Relationship Management is no longer considered a business trend, but an industry standard that is required to secure and maintain competitive advantage. When CRM is correctly and effectively utilized, results are always in positive terms like increase in profitability and customer loyalty. In view of considerable research and developments in web enabled CRM area during last two decades it becomes necessary to take stock of emerging technologies and identify emerging opportunities and bottlenecks in its implementations [2].

In this paper it is attempted to review developments in E-CRM that facilitates online service to customers. Apart from review of technology related developments, the study focuses on identification of thrust areas resulting benefits and implementation strategies. For the purpose of the study we have taken Almari Food Company as an example to show how this firm got success in achieving E-CRM by applying MIS.

2. Literature Review

There have been various attempts at building models of consumer behavior online. Examples include looking at "conversion" of Web surfers to Web customers [3], studying consumer information acquisition and purchase decision online [4], and determining reasons for not shopping online. Transaction cost theory has been used to explain the impact of IT on market structure but also to understand individual consumer behavior. For example, buyer search costs are substantial transaction costs and they can determine buyer behavior and eventually market structures [4]. An important question is whether online consumers think and act differently than their offline counterparts. If so, which metrics can we use to capture these differences? For example, online consumers cannot depend on all five senses to make purchases; instead, they must rely on limited product representations such as photographs and text descriptions. Yet, studies have shown that the representation of the product online, increase the overall quality of the shopping experience, matters for both attitude towards shopping online as well as intention to buy [5].

The online consumer may also have a different social and work environment than the offline consumer. For example, intention to buy online is influenced by the level of the consumer's lack of leisure time, as in offline shopping, but also by the level of their wired lifestyle [6]. A key difference between online and offline consumer behavior is that the online consumer is generally more powerful, demanding, and utilitarian in her shopping expeditions. As a result, customer loyalty on the Web is overall low [6]; although, as in the physical world, it is influenced by the availability of good, relevant content in an enjoyable context [7]. The locus of power seems to be shifting from the vendor to the consumer who does not favor traditional advertising and promotions online [8]. Research has also shown that certain site features, such as the availability of a FAQ section or promotions at the Web store entrance, can influence both traffic on the website and overall sales [8].

Unlike offline consumers, online consumers are concerned with those risks inherent in buying on the Web, risks such as credit card fraud and not receiving the right products [9]. Perceived risk of online shopping and perceived ease of use of the website have been shown to influence attitude towards online purchasing [9]. The impact of perceived ease of use, however, seems to vary depending on the type of task the consumer is undertaking. Its effect is more significant when consumers are using a website to inquire about products rather than to purchase those goods [9]. Online consumers clearly share some characteristics of their offline counterparts but also have unique needs and concerns that reflect their online environment. Our study examines some of those similarities and differences in B2C commerce. We concentrate on new customers of a Web store and we measure their emotional and cognitive responses to determine what influences their intention to return and unplanned purchases.

3. Discussion

This Study is a pilot research based on secondary data. For results a major dairy product's firm has been accounted namely Almarai foods in KSA. Annual reports are interpreted and inferences are made on various E-CRM standards and how this firm has been implementing in its respective ventures for consumers. Due to cultural hindrances personal in-depth interview could not be conducted. Data collected from financial journal was computed through Ratio Analysis and for comparative analysis Thurstone scale was used.

Three E-CRM parameters are composed through MIS which were used to know how these dairy firms got increase in customer retention and sales. Major source of data collection was through Almarai KSA's website [10].

During the early 1990s, Almarai entered a period of restructuring and reinvestment that took it from a decentralized structure to a centralized structure. The aim was to establish as a low-cost producer so that the consumers can enjoy high-quality products at an affordable price [7].

In line with this model, Almarai replaced five decentralized processing plants with its first central processing plant. It also replaced ten small decentralized dairy farms with four large dairy farms in Al Kharj in the central region.

In late 2005, Almarai commissioned a second, larger central processing plant, incorporating a new cheese plant. It also commissioned two new super-farms. In the same year, it was moved from being a privately owned company to a publicly listed company and now it has around 50,000 shareholders. At the end of 2016, its market capitalization exceeded SAR23 billion. Paving the way for geographical expansion beyond GCC, the firm pooled its respective expertise in dairy and juice with PepsiCo. In 2009, it also launched a joint venture with the International Dairy and Juice (IDJ) Company. Today, Almarai is capable of delivering high quality of products to more than 100,000 customers within the Gulf Cooperation Council (GCC), Egypt and Jordan daily [7]. Figure 1 shows the product mix of Almarai.

Figure 1. Product Mix Almarai [7-10].

The firm analyzed customer's survey and reviews on social media and tried to innovate and add value to its product mix. Almarai has always focused on values for price and used MIS for evaluating customer willingness to pay for the dairy products. Figure 2 shows the customer choice for Almarai over other competitive brands.

The results clearly show that none of the competitor has major preference over Almarai. MIS conducted a survey to show the results of best brands in KSA, this survey was not based on product related firms rather over all comparison in terms of organizations' contribution for benefitting society especially in the amid of COVID-19. Figure 3 presents the success of Almari and provides evidence of success use of MIS in E-CRM [10].

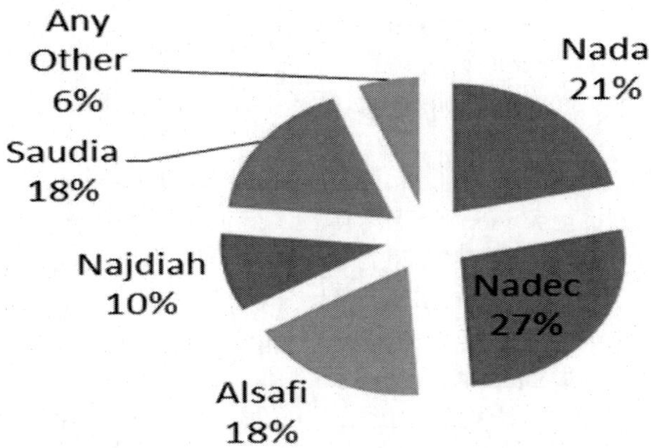

Figure 2. Percentage of Customer Choice for Almarai [8].

BEST BRANDS 2020 IN SAUDI ARABIA		
Rank	**Brand Name**	**Score**
1	Almarai	50.0
2	Al Baik	49.1
3	Saudia (Saudi Airlincs)	47.5
4	mada	43.7
5	YouTube	43.3
6	WhatsApp	41.7
7	Google	41.7
8	Dettol	41.1
9	Apple	40.8
10	Samsung	39.6

Figure 3. Best Brands in the Saudi Arabia in the year 2020 [10].

Relevance of social media cannot be overlooked in the digital scenario, therefore Almari measured its performance on facebook, and Table 1 shows the list of features applied for the appraisal.

Table 1. Evaluation of Facebook page for CRM [11]

Features used for evaluation of CRM on Facebook
Front Page
About
Activity
Response

Firms from different sectors are selected to show the results of features considered. It is important to note that these firms are not directly competitors of the firm Almarai. Figure 4 shows the results from facebook as major success for all the features of CRM.

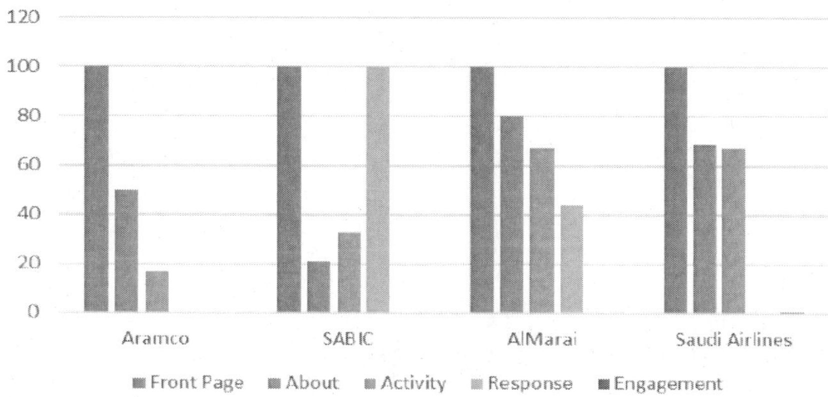

Figure 4. Evaluation of Facebook for selected firms [9] [10].

For measuring CRM some important factors have to be evaluated, Almarai applied MIS to know about customer preferences and used E-CRM for its customers and the results show high satisfaction levels. Figure 5 shows the increase in satisfaction for Almarai products offering and value for money. All the factors are showing high scores for the ECRM.

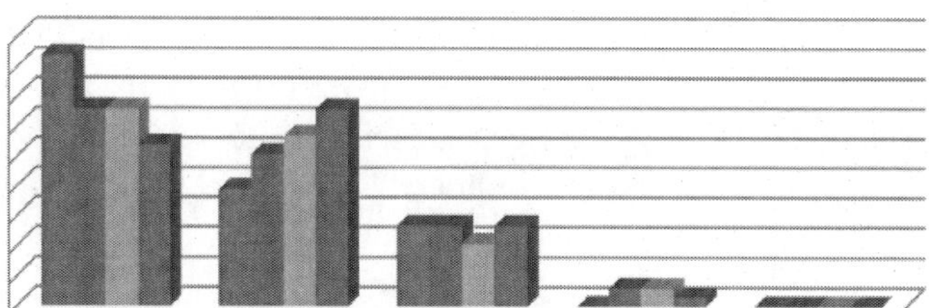

	Satisfactory	Somewhat Satisfactory	Very Satisfactory	Somewhat Dissatisfactory	Dissatisfactory
Overall Quality	84	39	27	0	0
Value that you get	66	51	27	6	0
Purchase Experience	66	57	21	6	0
Usage Experience	54	66	27	3	0

Figure 5. Performance of products through satisfaction [11].

Almarai has been a leader in applying new technologies and MIS for managing and delivering the services to the customers. Figure 6 show the areas contributing for the success of MIS for Almarai.

Figure 6. Consultation field of MIS for Almarai [11].

Figure 7 presents the contribution of different levels of Almarai to enhance the image and quality of services for the firm. In the current scenario with the application of MIS, the firm is able to offer excellent product quality, strengthen the brand image, achieve market leadership and acquire world-class capabilities. Figure 7 shows a simple list of achievement of Almrai for ECRM.

MIS in general scenario works for facilitating the organizations for achieving strategic leadership and to accomplish this the firms have to perform many successful tasks on various levels. Out of these the most important is to achieve customer satisfaction and build CRM. Almrai has also applied MIS for achieving strategic leadership and works for all the levels. Past 5 years Almarai focused more on ECRM for customer satisfaction. Figure 8 shows the implication of MIS for Almarai for strategic leadership and providing improved and innovated products for ECRM.

Figure 7. Success factors of Almarai [12].

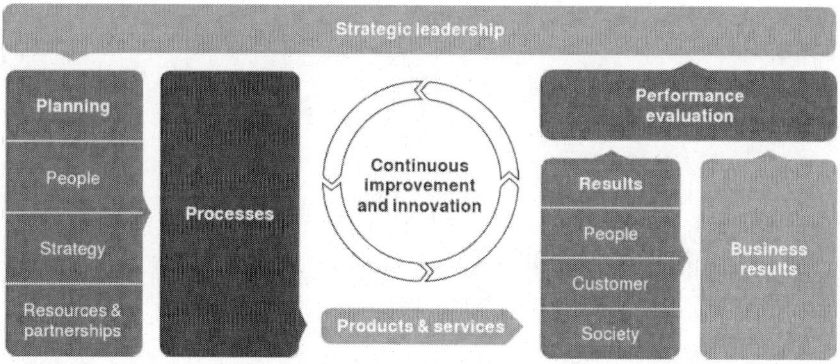

Figure 8. MIS for Almarai for continuous improvement and innovation [12].

4. Results

For Almarai foods results showed 25% of increase in sales from 2004 to 2009 and continued till 2013 and after implication of E-CRM standards the firms show 50% growth. It is noteworthy here that Almarai is the largest food company in KSA therefore it should have applied Multichannel E-CRM, since 2020 the firm has started to apply and future results will show the real impact but for now the firm is having increasing curve for sales and ECRM practices. Till the date it is still on the way to develop good ECRM unit for the firm. Like its Strategic Alliance Pepsi Food in US has developed multichannel ECRM and showed drastic sales and customer satisfaction too. Back in 2009, Almarai had started an initiative called "Almarai for Innovation Management" which is at the center of its innovation activities. Almarai's research and development efforts annually result in testing of 630 experimental products each year with 65 products under development at all times throughout the year. More than 60 new products were launched in 2018 & 2019 under different categories by the application of MIS and for achieving ECRM.

Conclusion

ECRM is no longer considered a business trend, but an industry standard that is required to secure and maintain competitive advantage and when correctly utilized, it results in increase in profitability and greater customer loyalty. The applications of ECRM have resulted in positive results for Almarai, KSA, the firm is able to achieve highest market share, rise in sales and consumer retention after E-CRM implementation.

References

[1] Talón-Ballestero, P., González-Serrano, L., Soguero-Ruiz, C., Munoz-Romero, S., & Rojo-Álvarez, J. L. (2018). Using big data from customer relationship management information systems to determine the client profile in the hotel sector. *Tourism Management*, 68, 187-197.

[2] Heim, G. R., Meile, L., Tease, J., Glass, J., Laher, S., Rowan, J., & Comerford, K. (2005). Experiential learning in a management information systems course: Simulating IT consulting and CRM system procurement. *Communications of the Association for Information Systems*, 15(1), 25.

[3] Kim, H. W., & Pan, S. L. (2006). Towards a process model of information systems implementation: the case of customer relationship management (CRM). *ACM SIGMIS Database: The DATABASE for Advances in Information Syst*ems, 37(1), 59-76.

[4] Naim, A. (2018). Strategies to Achieve Students' Centric Approach in Blended Learning. *International Journal of Engineering and Management Research (IJEMR),* 8(2), 214-219.

[5] Ku, E. C. (2010). The impact of customer relationship management through implementation of information systems. *Total Quality Management,* 21(11), 1085-1102.

[6] Chen, Y., & Li, L. (2006). Deriving information from CRM for knowledge management—a note on a commercial bank. Systems Research and Behavioral Science: *The Official Journal of the International Federation for Systems Research,* 23(2), 141-146.

[7] Naim, A., Khan, M. F., Hussain, M. R., & Khan, N. (2019). "Virtual Doctor" Management Technique in the Diagnosis of ENT Diseases. *JOE,* 15(9), 88.

[8] Arab, F., Selamat, H., & Zamani, M. (2010, September). An overview of success factors for CRM. In *2010 2nd IEEE International Conference on Information and Financial Engineering* (pp. 702-705). IEEE.

[9] Naim, A., Sattar, R. A., Al Ahmary, N.., & Razwi, M. T. (2021) Implementation of Quality Matters Standards on Blended Courses: A Case Study. *FINANCE INDIA Indian Institute of Finance* Vol. XXXV No. 3, September 2021 Pages—873 – 890.

[10] Singh, A., & Hagahmoodi, S. O. (2017). Performance Measurement of Almarai Products and Customer Satisfaction. *International Journal of Management Science*, 4(1), 1-12.

[11] Sadi, M. A. (2006). Case study: marketing perspective of Almarai dairy food company. *International Journal of Management Cases*, 9(1), 42-50.

[12] Lotayif, M. S. (2017). Causality Relationships between Main Branding Variables and International Marketing Strategy: Evidence from MNCs in GCC Market. *International Journal of Business and Managem*ent, 12(1).

[13] Mohamad, K. A., & Asfour, A. M. (2020). Is the Business in Saudi Market Sustainable, Case Study of Almarai. *IIUM Journal of Case Studies in Management*, 11(2), 7-14.

[14] Osland, A. (2021). *Saudi Arabia: Almarai and Vision 2030*. SAGE Publications: SAGE Business Cases Originals.

[15] AL Zubaidi, A., & Nobanee, H. (2020). Performance Analysis of Almarai. *Haitham, Performance Analysis of Almarai* (August 16, 2020).

[16] Khan, N., Naim, A., Hussain, M. R., Naveed, Q. N., Ahmad, N., & Qamar, S. (2019, May). The 51 v's of big data: survey, technologies, characteristics,

opportunities, issues and challenges. In *Proceedings of the international conference on omni-layer intelligent s*ystems (pp. 19-24).

[17] Naim, A., & Alahmari, F. (2020). Reference model of e-learning and quality to establish interoperability in higher education systems. *International Journal of Emerging Technologies in Learning (iJET)*, 15(2), 15-28.

[18] Guerola-Navarro, V., Oltra-Badenes, R., Gil-Gomez, H., & Gil-Gomez, J. A. (2021). Research model for measuring the impact of customer relationship management (CRM) on performance indicators. *Economic Research-Ekonomska Istraživanja*, 34(1), 2669-2691.

[19] Naim, A. (2020). Realization of diverse Electronic tools in learning and teaching for students with diverse skills. *Global Journal of Enterprise Information System*, 12(1), 72-78.

[20] Svoboda, P., Ghazal, T. M., Afifi, M. A., Kalra, D., Alshurideh, M. T., & Alzoubi, H. M. (2021, June). Information Systems Integration to Enhance Operational Customer Relationship Management in the Pharmaceutical Industry. *In The International Conference on Artificial Intelligence and Computer Vision* (pp. 553-572). Springer, Cham.

[21] Khlif, H. (2021). Factors for Success in Customer Relationship Management (CRM) Systems. *World Academics Journal of Management*, 9(1), 16-20.

[22] Naim, A., Hussain, M. R., Naveed, Q. N., Ahmad, N., Qamar, S., Khan, N., & Hweij, T. A. (2019, April). Ensuring interoperability of e-learning and quality development in education. In *2019 IEEE Jordan International Joint Conference on Electrical Engineering and Information Technology (JEEIT)* (pp. 736-741). IEEE.

[23] Tien, N. H., Diem, P. T., Vu, N. T., Dung, H. T., Bien, B. X., Duc, P. M., & Van Dat, N. (2021). Customer care and customer relationship maintenance at Ministop, FamilyMart and CoopSmile in Vietnam. *International journal multidisciplinary research and growth evaluation,* 2(4), 744-751.

[24] Naim, A., Alahmari, F., & Rahim, A. (2021). Role of Artificial Intelligence in Market Development and Vehicular Communication. *Smart Antennas: Recent Trends in Design and Applications*, 2, 28.

Chapter 3

Applications of Green Information Technologies in Business Process Management

Arshi Naim*

Department of Information Systems, King Khalid University,
Abha, Kingdom of Saudi Arabia (KSA)

Abstract

Green computing is also called as Green Information Technologies (GIT) which is the practice and procedures of using computing and other technological resources in a responsible and environmental friendly manner. Climatic changes have raised the concern worldwide and countries are conducting summits to solve and prevent global warming. Information Technologies have been playing the great roles in keeping the objectives of preserving environment and one of the techniques is to apply Green computing. The focus of GIT is to decrease the use of hazardous materials, reduce usage of energy, increase profit maximization and create the awareness of advantages of recyclability or biodegradability of the computer trash. This paper presents the theoretical background of GIT, its roles and advantages for preserving climate. Also this chapter presents qualitative analysis on advantages and challenges of using GIT in business operations (BPO). These advantages are presented through very short instances and cases for the applications of GIT in BPO. GIT includes new services and products with optimum

* Corresponding Author's Email: arshi@kku.edu.sa.

In: Competitive Trends and Technologies in Business Management
Editors: Arshi Naim and Praveen K. Malik
ISBN: 978-1-68507-612-2

efficiency andpossible options towards energy saving so it provides the best way to keep the environment clean and healthy without trading off the use of technologies.

Keywords: green computing, GIT, recycle, computer trash, business operations

1. Introduction

In the absence of GIT, increase in energy consumption would lead to increase in carbon dioxide and other negative effects on climate. GIT studies the use of the computers and other technology in eco- friendly way for all types of BPO in such a way that the relevance of technologies remains same and firms achieves the profit maximization too [1]. In the current scenario, life without electronics gadgets and devices seem difficult and to an extent impossible. Therefore it is important to discuss the consequences of using technologies on environment and explaining the advantages of GIT for the future of Earth. There is several life saving benefits GIT has encouraged BPO to apply in their practices. Some of the disadvantages for not using GIT are given in the Figure 1.

Firms for their BPO using GIT can reduce energy consumption of computing and other resources, save energy during idle operation, apply options for eco-friendly sources of energy, reduce harmful effects of computing resources, reduces computing wastes, etc. This approach will help to seek solutions to reduce climatic changes and prevent global warming. This will reduce the flood and famine and other natural disasters on the globe. Also GIT applications can increase the effective use of power and reduce the computing wastes. However the option of GIT is not always cost effective, firms using GIT for their BPO have to increase their investment but at the stake of climate preservation this decision is mandatory [2].

It is witnessed that in the past decades the IT has not only changed our lives and increased the standard of living but also have impacted the businesses and increased their productivity. In the current situation IT has challenging roles to play, it provides benefits for all sectors and for the applications of green concepts. This challenge rather responsibility of IT is vital because in a greater sense IT is held accountable for many environmental issues. Devices and other IT equipment's have increased the usage of power and created a heavy pressure on electricity grid. Not only this, IT has also increased the pollution in water, land and air by increasing its technological disposes [2]. In this paper researchers have discussed the problems aggravated by IT and how GIT can bring possible solutions. It is important to apply IT in an innovative ways to check the increasing problems of environment and motivate to use GIT at all levels of BPM. GIT is the study and practice of designing, manufacturing and using computers and communications systems efficiently and effectively, with zero or minimal impact on the environment. It is the responsibility of the organizations to adopt a policy of GIT to ensure that the setup and operations of IT produces the least CO_2. GIT is also about using IT to support, assist other environmental initiatives and to help create green awareness. GIT includes devices such as hardware, software, tools, and practices that improve environmental sustainability. GIT benefits the environment by improving energy efficiency, using less harmful materials and encouraging reuse and recycling. As business and government try to balance the growth with environmental risks, GIT can help in different ways to improve our environmental sustainability [3].

This research is divided into three parts. First part is a Literature Review which will cover the theoretical background of GIT, its generations and approaches. Second part will discuss in detail about the GIT applications, types, challenges and advantages of GIT in BPO. Third part will show the results of application of GIT in BPO through short instances.

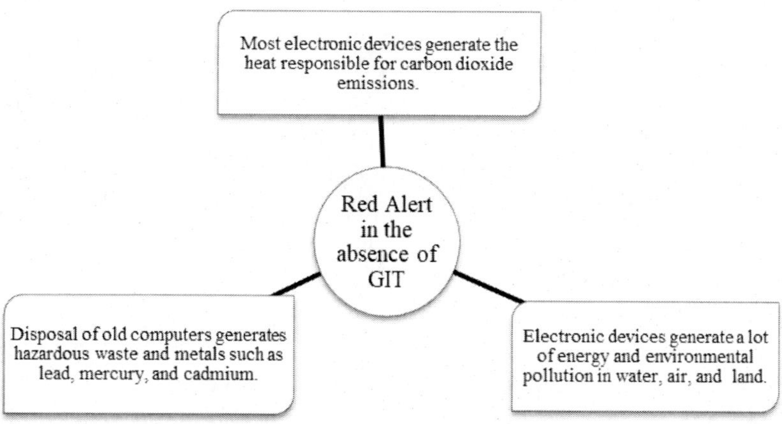

Figure 1. Consequences of not using GIT [1].

2. Literature Review

In the 90s decade, US EPA launched the Energy Star (ES) focusing on GIT. ES was a program installed to the computers and other electronic devices to save energy consumption. ES created the sleep mode or standby mode on a computer when it is on but not being used. This program was able to minimize the use of the energy and maximize the efficiency of the devices [4]. In the later years ES enhanced its features and called as Green Computing or GIT. With the growth of GIT, many countries joined together to pursue BPO with GIT. Swedish organization TCO launched the TCO Certification program to promote low magnetic and electrical emissions from CRT based computer's display. It was later expanded to include criteria on energy consumption and the use of hazardous materials in construction. This was the major step of using GIT at global level.

In late 90s, the United Nations' Kyoto Protocol mandated the reduction of carbon emissions and required manufacturers to calculate the electricity used by the computers. The Climate Savers Computing was created to try to reduce the amount of electric power computer use in last years of 2000s.

From past studies we can know, how IT has impacted the environment, it is found that each stage of a computer's life, from its production, through its use and to its disposal, impacts environment adversely. Since late 90s consumption of IT based BPO has increased and firms manufacturing computers and their various electronic and non-electronic components consume more electricity, raw materials, chemicals and water, and eventually generate dangerous wastes harming the environment. All these BPO directly or indirectly increase CO_2 emissions and affect the environment. Each computer devices or other electronic inputs generate tons of CO_2 every year and this rate is increasing since 2007 [5]. It is found that total electrical energy consumption by servers, computers, monitors, and data communications equipment is increasing every year twice than the previous year resulting in greater CO_2 emissions.

Computer components contain toxic materials and consumers discard a large number of old computers, monitors and other electronic equipment in 3–5 years after purchase, and most of these usually end up in a landfill. Most electronics contain non-biodegradable materials, and heavy metals and toxic materials like cadmium, lead, and mercury. Over the period of time, these toxic materials have leaked into the ground, where they can contaminate the water that people drink, the plants for food and the animals that live around the area [5]. These toxic materials can cause all kinds of bad effects including nausea, diarrhea, vomiting and even fatal diseases like cancer. The increased number of computers and their use, along with their frequent replacements, create major concern for environment. Consequently, there is increasing pressure on the IT industry and businesses to make IT environmental friendly throughout its life cycle. In the year 2007, climatic changes pushed to implement the GIT for all types of BPO, where GIT referred as the information technologies systems, applications and practices that encompass three dimensions to improve environmental sustainability and preserve nature [6].

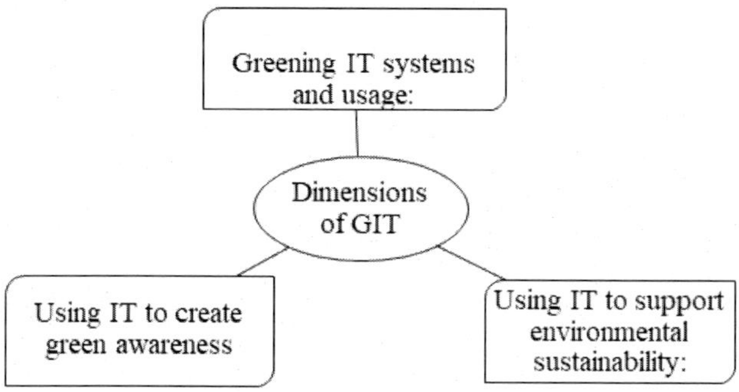

Figure 2. Three dimensions of GIT [6].

GIT explains the roles and advantages of IT for environment for various benefits, in past one decade GIT insists on using efficient and effective design, use and disposal of computer hardware in eco- friendly manner, software and communication systems with no or minimal impact on the environment. Also GIT encourages the firms to apply the concept not only for a particular BPO but at the enterprise level. Stakeholders and other role players in the business are required to follow the GIT and promote the eco-friendly BPO [6].

In 2007 to 2009, world submit discussed the role of GIT for higher levels of applications and introduced the generation Green IT 1.0, that explained to reduce the emissions of Greenhouse gases (GHG) by reducing the release of CO_2 but only this measure was not enough to prevent climatic changes. Therefore second generation of GIT 2.0 was introduced in late 2009, GIT 2.0 focused on IT for green concept. This approach revised 1.0 application and explained the application of GIT covering all the sectors of businesses. GIT 2.0 was externally focused and empowered the range of other green initiatives aimed at reducing environmental degradation and reducing CO_2 emissions. Figure 3 shows the wider benefits and coverage of GIT 2.0.

In the year 2010, GIT addressed more options of applications for BPO and suggested six directions for more green advantages. Firms were instructed to apply these options for all the levels of BPO. Figure 4 shows the six directions of GIT that firms can follow for their BPO.

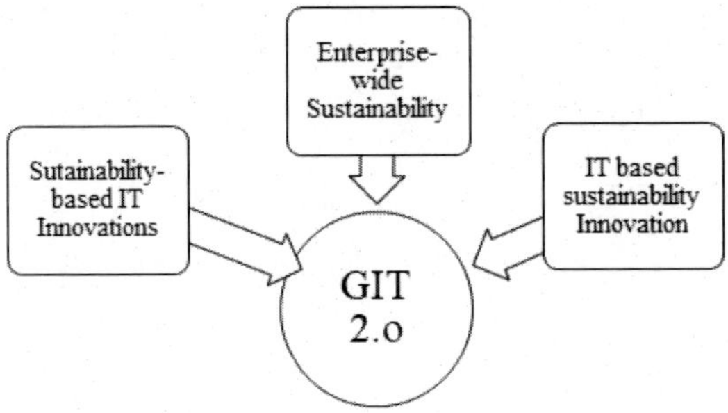

Figure 3. GIT 2.0 Coverage [7].

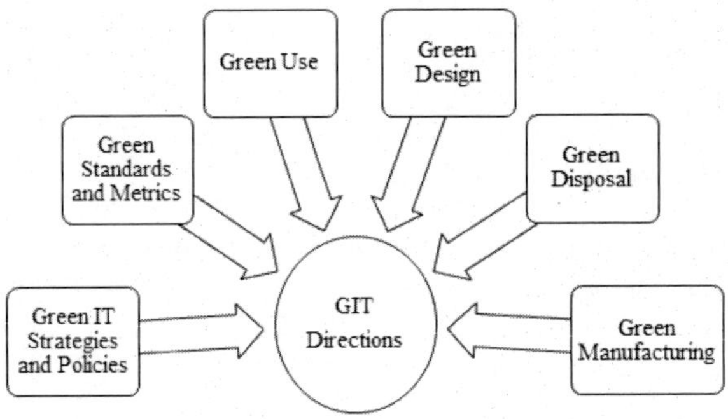

Figure 4. Directions of GIT for BPO [8].

These six directions of GIT, explained the options and methods for the firms for going green. Some of these methods are design energy-efficient and environmentally sound components, computers, servers, cooling equipment, manufacturing electronic components, computers and other associated subsystems with minimal or no impact on the environment. Also GIT directions encouraged the green use by reducing the energy consumption of computers and other information systems,using them in eco- friendly manner, disposing the unwanted computers and other hardware in a right manner without causing danger and pollution to land, water and air. GIT suggested the firms to apply three Rs in their BPO, which are to reuse, refurbish and recycle [8]. In the year 2015, GIT established benchmarking and strategies to promote more echo- friendly IT techniques for BPO and constantly monitored the firms for their practices, if they are affecting the environment or preserving the nature. Figure 5, shows the GIT application for the BPO process and outlines how it can reduce the toxic released in environment.

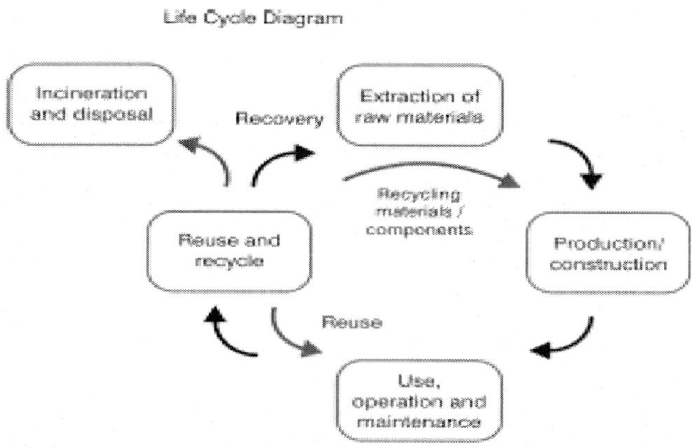

Figure 5. GIT Life-cycle [9].

Past sixty years Organization for Economic Co-operation and Development (OECD) produced independent analysis and statistics to promote policies to improve economic and social wellbeing across the globe. (OECD) has proposed a green IT framework consisting of three analytical levels for IT based firms and for general business scenario.

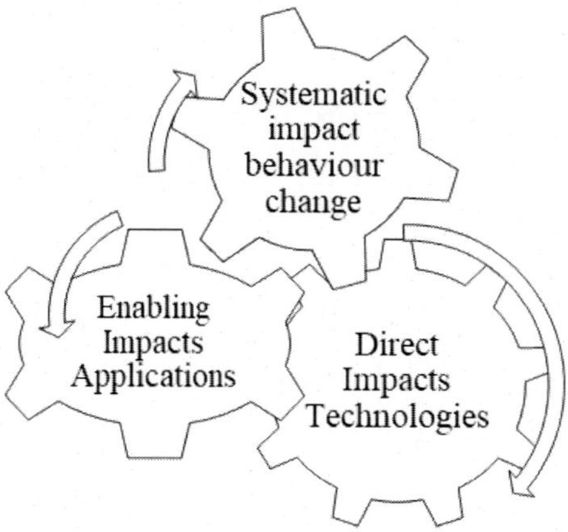

Figure 6. OCED GIT frameworks [9].

3. Discussion

GIT proposes various IT based solutions to BPO for the successful application and achieving profit maximization as well as contributes to the society for future preservation.

Multithreading (MLT) contributes in GIT for BPO by delivering performance with better energy efficiency. MLT is the ability of CPU or a single core in a multi core processor to execute multiple processes or threads concurrently, appropriately supported by the operating system, therefore application of MLT in GIT facilitates in completing the workload while consuming less energy. GIT suggests using MLT over single thread technologies (SNT) because the MLT uses about 25% less energy than the SNT [10]. A well-balanced MLT workload is more energy efficient than running the same workload with a SNT. Besides MLT can complete the process one fourth time faster than SNT and leaves the processor for other processes.

Another application that GIT encourages the firms to use in its processes is Virtualization (Vn), which is a term used when creating a virtual environment for any program to run on an existing platform as a guest, without interfering or interrupting with the host platform's servicesor programs. The virtual environment running might be an operating system, network or an application server among other things. Figure 8 shows the structure of traditional and virtual applications.

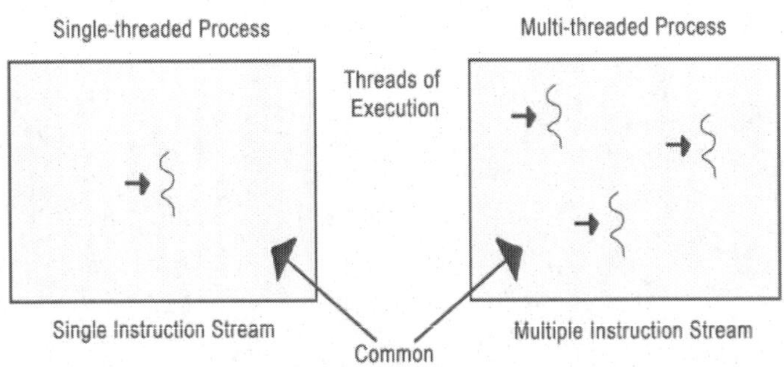

Figure 7. MLT vs. SNT operations [11].

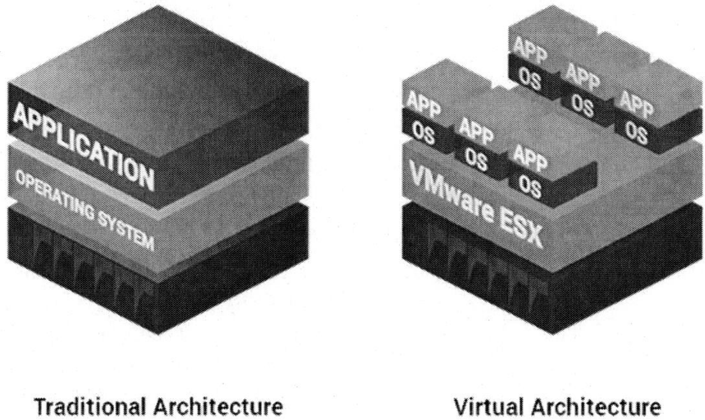

Figure 8. Traditional Architecture and Virtual Architecture [12].

GIT suggests using types of Vn for BPO and for IT based applications, these are Software Virtualization (S/wVn), Network Virtualization (NVn) and Desktop Virtualization (DVn)

S/wVN involves the creation an operation of multiple virtual environments on the host machine. It creates a complete computer system with hardware that lets the guest operating system to run. For example, it lets Android OS to run on a host machine natively using a Microsoft Windows OS, utilizing the same hardware as the host machine does. In NVn, there are two or more virtual networks can be created within the same physical network belonging to the same IP range and yet they do not have the authorization to communicate with each other. They operate in their own logical network, with each logical network having a different set of processes and functions to perform. They are segregated withinthe same physical network. DVn enables to remotely access the data from anywhere and anytime through any device. It provides flexibility and feasibility for employees and the data is safe and secure as it is stored at a centralized location. All three types of Vn are aiding GIT in using the effective and efficient power and energy for completing the processes.

Other technological options that firms can apply for their BPO are Power Management (Pmgnt), Storage Consolidation (StC), Solar Energy Computing (SEC), etc. Pmgnt allows an operating system to directly control the power saving for the hardware devices. This allows a system to automatically turn off the components like monitors and hard drives after set periods of inactivity. In addition, a system may hibernate, where most components including the

CPU and the system RAM are turned off. Besides some CPUs can automatically under volt the processor depending on the workload, this technology is termed as Speed-step introduced by Intel. StC offers allow consolidating data onto a centralized storage system and making the data center more efficient. Direct attached storage, has multiple disk drives in every server, results in difficulty to manage storage with low utilization levels. Each isolated disk drive consumes power and contributes to the waste stream when the server is ultimately replaced. The centralized storage allows managing storage and servers independently, allowing matching the storage hardware to the data requirements. SEC plays the most critical role in GIT technology, as the use of SEC reduces the emission of heat and other harmful gases such as CO_2. In SEC for GIT, cells are used in the large panel and solar cells require very little maintenance after installation. There is no further cost for many years so it is cost effective also for businesses. Also SEC devices are manufactured with non-polluted inputs, and are efficient, silent and highly reliable. SEC is echo friendly because during the production of this energy no toxicmaterials or gases are evolved which can harm the atmosphere [13].

There are many GIT Applications for effective BPO; Figure 9 shows the list of some of them.

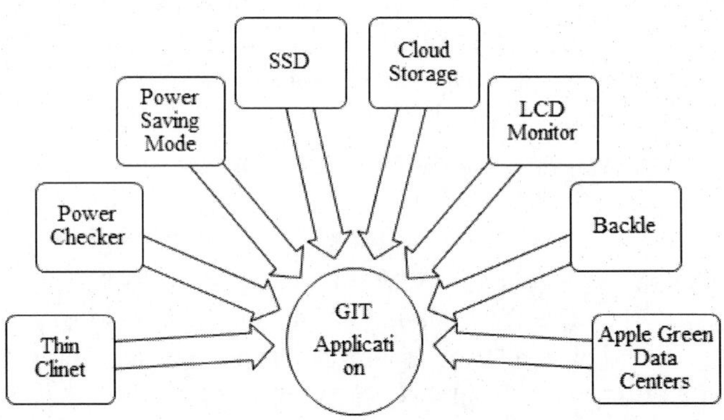

Figure 9. List of GIT Applications [13].

Cloud storage is a cloud computing model in which data is stored on remote servers accessed from the internet. It is maintained, operated and managed by a cloud storage service provider on storage servers that are built on Vn techniques. In addition to simply using less power due to less physical H/w, larger companies can reduce their energy consumption and will reduce annual carbon emissions to the equivalent of nearly 200 million barrels of oil each year. Some of the green cloud storage services include Google Drive, Mega and iCloud [14].

Blackle is a search-engine site powered by Google custom search which aims to save energy bydisplaying a black background and using grayish-white font color for search results. The results of searches from Google show that if everyone switched from Google to Blackle, 750MW power can be saved each year.

Apple recently announced it has achieved a complete reliance on renewable energy sources for all its data centers. Data centers that house computing infrastructure for services like iTunes, Siri, Maps and the App Store now get 100% of their power from a combination of renewable energy [15].

Most devices and operating systems support many power saving modes such as screen savers. This mode allows the screen to enter a dormant state after a certain period of inactivity.Sleep mode control causes the screen to turn off after a certain period of inactivity. This mode provides a large amount of power saving and contributes in echo- friendly aspects. There is also the hard disk sleep mode, but the amount of power provided in this mode is not much. Standby mode stops all computer components after a period of sleep. This mode is characterized by rapid retrieval of the system at reboot, so this is the best method of comfort for the user and the preservation of the environment, but the amount of energy consumed by the computer in this situation is not as few as 5 watts. The latest situation that the systems currently support is hibernation, which takes an additional step compared to the standby mode, where it loads the memory onto the hard drive and stops all components of the computer. This is the best method in terms of the amount of energy consumed up to 3 watts, but it takes longer time to reboot, because it needs to load the memory from the hard disk first, and then restore the system. Operating systems and devices have generally supported different modes to save energy [16].

SSD storage device uses integrated circuit assemblies as memory to store data persistently. SSD is more energy efficient than an HDD and by replacing hard drives with solid- state computer can save 10 percent off their energy.

Thin Client is a lightweight computer that doesn't have a hard drive but connects to a server to perform its computing and because it does not have hard driver, it does not need maintenance, backup, upgrades or hardware upgrades, and its virtual life is about twice as long as the PC also thin clients use very little energy because most of the processing is done on the server. Thin clients are environmental friendly because they have less hardware so they generate less-waste at the end of their lifecycles. One example of thin client computer is Sunray Thin Client. Sun Ray consumes 4 to 8 wattsof power because most of the heavy computation is performed by a server. Sunrays are particularly well suited for cost-sensitive environments such as call centers, education, healthcare, service providers, and finance [17].

LCD monitors typically use a cold-cathode fluorescent bulb to provide light for the display. Some newer displays use an array of light-emitting diodes (LEDs) in place of the fluorescent bulb, which reduces the amount of electricity used by the display. LCD monitors uses three times less when active, and ten times less energy when in sleep mode. LCDs are up to 66% more energy efficient than CRTs. LCDs are 80% smaller in size and weight therefore lead to fuel savings in shipping and transportation. LCDs produce less heat which means they need less Air Condition to keep the devices cool. LCD screens are also easier on the eyes. Their lower intensity and steady light pattern result in less fatigue than CRTs.

Table 1. Features of GIT for BPO [18]

Less use of Dangerous Elements
Energy Efficiency
Recycled Materials Used for Manufacturing
End of Life Recovery
Use of Renewable and Bio-Based Materials
Longer Life
End of Life Take-back Facility
Manufacturer's Certification

Table 2. List of Challenges for BPO [18]

Return on Investment
Disposal of Electronic Wastes
Cost
Design

The Intel-developed Power Checker tool that helped software developers to measure software energy efficiency and write energy-aware software. Energy-aware software is able to measure and report dynamically its energy efficiency metrics. The Power Informer tool was designed to simplify this task, so the software vendor can focus on developing the heuristics required to save energy.

Referring to many case studies on GIT, it was found that if firms use the basic features of GIT in their routine and special BPO, energy can be saved, minimal waste and reduce emission of CO2 and can bring good return on investment to the firms also. Table 1 shows some of the features of GIT that have been extensively applied by many businesses in manufacturing and other operations.

A lot of dangerous substances are used in the production of acomputer ranging from the more lethal ones like cadmium, lead, chromium, and mercury to the relatively less dangerous ones like flame retardants, pesticides, and chlorinated plastics. GIT components should ideally be completely free of these lethal substances. Energy Efficiency is one of the features of GIT that pleases not only the environmental enthusiasts but also the budget-conscious buyer. The GIT is designed in such a way that at the end of their life their components can be easily reused, disassembled, or recycled. Another of the important GIT feature is the increased use of renewable or bio-based materials. GIT come in modular and upgradeable designs with the idea of extending their life cycle. GIT should come with a take-back policy, where the manufacturer offer the provisions to take back the computer at the end of its life and offer the buyer a new purchase at a competitive price. Hence, it is mandatory to verify the brand of GIT in buying or taking back. Before settle on a particular brand of green computers, buyers should ensure that its manufacturer has ISO-14001 certification, which is the bare minimum for a manufacturer to qualify as environmental-policy compliant. GIT has several advantages and its applications have made mandatory by the global policies for all the business owners for their BPO. However it is found that applying GIT is not easy rather a challenging tasks for all firms for various reasons. Table 2, has listed some of the challenges of GIT for BPO.

Return on Investment is the major problem for educating the stakeholders regarding the environmental impact of computers. Also, one drawback of GIT applications in the BPO is that firms cannot demonstrate immediate results. For a BPO that involves Greening, the returns are generally seen after a long period of time. Hence an important challenge in any BPO is to show the immediate returns after the successful implementation of GIT. Reliability about the use of GIT in BPO is perhaps the biggest single challenge faced by the industries. They are likely to be free of hazardous materials such as brominates flame-retardants and heavy metals such as lead, cadmium, and mercury, which are commonly, used in computer manufacturing. Replacements like copper/silver alloy also require higher melting temperatures, which can affect chip life. Use of GIT in BPO always adds extra investments because replacement of present inputs requires innovative technologies to prevent the emission of CO_2 and to reduce the wastes. Designing with GIT is another challenge faced by the BPO because it has to ensure the design side, energy efficiency in focusing on less power consumption, retaining performance. This is not a simple process because it demands high levels of skilled engineering.

GIT does more for the business dynamic than merely helping the environment. From financial boosts to productivity, firms may find a lot of benefits by adopting a "green" platform [19]. In reality, there are several green products that benefit the workplace outside of protecting the environment. Reducing Energy Bills is one of the most benefits of GIT at the workplace because it reduces the energy bills and operating costs. Small changes such as using LED lighting can save some money in operational costs each month. Energy efficiency can be implemented in many ways from the insulation of the building to smart windows that offer shade when ultraviolet levels increase. Through eco-friendly technology and affordable additions, firm could easily reduce the amount of the overhead costs. Reducing Water Use, while water may be cheap in some areas, technology can be utilized to reduce the use of this component in the workplace. Bathrooms, drinking fountains and gardening are three of the most common uses of water in many businesses. Aerated faucets, efficient toilets and outdoor timing systems could greatly cut into the monthly water bills. Many companies will install motion-sensing faucets which will automatically turn off when no movement is detected. Some businesses have been able to reduce water waste by more than half because of the applications like sensor-based appliances [20]. Less Waste in the Workplace, many organizations pay for the amount of trash that is discarded each month. A lot of these businesses will also pay for paper-shredding services such as insurance companies and those who process confidential information. Moving to a paperless system eliminates a large portion of the waste in the workplace. This has the potential to save money in those services as well as reducing the company's carbon footprint. Moving to a Green Web Host, having a website for your business is essential for success. Reducing general office expenses, utilizing more GIT in the business will also reduce general office supply expenses. While paper may be the most obvious product, take into consideration including spending for pens, paperclips, markers, etc can be reduced by moving into a digital platform [21].

Improving Productivity in the Workplace, Many eco-friendly pieces of technology also deliver improvements for productivity. For example, it's much easier to find digital documents on the Cloud than to sift through a filing cabinet.

Mobile devices, messaging systems and even appliances that improve air quality can make an impact in how people perform their jobs. This increase could lead to additional revenues depending on the types of services the company delivers. Improving Budgets for Greater Income, moving to a green platform has great potential to save money across the board. These savings can then be utilized in other aspects of the business to generate even more revenue [22].

For example, firm can use the money it saves on electricity bills to improve marketing or product enhancements in a store. It may be possible to reinvest that money for other facets that could improve the business even further such as hiring additional staff or investing more in social media [23].

Improving Employee Health, is one of the most effective benefits in the workplace from eco-friendly technology is the aspect of improving employee health. Air quality, temperate climate and other factors can lead to staff calling in sick.

This causes a trickle-down effect that makes the business less productive throughout the day. Air purifiers, proper air filtration on HVAC systems and more can offer a healthier workplace [24]. Even the thought of working in a better environment could improve employee morale, which often leads to greater productivity. Improved Disaster Recovery, GIT could help the organization recover from even the most devastating of disasters [25].

4. Results

This part of the paper shows short examples of successful firms which are world leaders because they have applied GIT in their BPO. They tried to find the solutions for all the challenges and benefitted the society by the applications of Green products. Some of the examples are discussed briefly in this paper as results.

Intel is known as the world's manufacturer of computer processors. It takes the lead in using green energy of up to 3,100,000,000 k. Intel use GIT and its green energy is drawn from sources including wind, solar, hydro, and biomass which has 18 on-site solar panels which generate electricity capacity of 7,000 kW. Intel Company uses the GIT to power its electric operation requirements in the manufacture and processing of processors as well as other computer accessories. The company intends to continue expanding and developing more renewable energy sources so that it can operate on 100% green energy [25].

Apple may not be the largest consumer of green energy but is among the top tech companies utilizing this energy option efficiently. Apple's use of GIT is placed at about 635,000,000 kWh annually. Just like Intel Company, Apple uses green energy to power its electric operation requirements in the manufacture and processing of its technology products including laptops, monitors, smartphones, and smartwatches. Apple's use of GIT is inspired by the fact that it has the objective of having a neutral carbon footprint. It has acquired numerous solar farms to ensure its data centers are sustainable [25]. Apple also works towards making its entire stores 100% energy efficient by the use of GIT. Apple is very keen on having a good image, whether it comes to its products or how they operate. Therefore, it is unsurprising to see that it is working hard to be as green as they can be. The company states to be the only company which runs its data centers through 100% renewable energy and also has a product range which exceeds the ES guidelines. The company has the goal of powering all of its stores and offices with renewable energy and as of 2013 it had reached 73%, with expectations to reach 100% in the current year [25].

Dell is keen to decrease the energy requirements of its data centers and hardware and has been working to reduce its environmental impact. The company has been one of the leading innovators in the tech sector when it comes to packaging and recycling and in 2014 the company launched its '2020 Legacy of Good' plan. In the plan, the company has set goals to reduce greenhouse gas emissions from its facilities and logistics operations, as well as reducing the energy intensity of its product portfolio by 80%. Dell, one of the leading companies in monitor and laptop manufacturing, also falls in this list because it works towards making the world a better place by using energy from sustainable sources to power its electrical operation needs. The company has heavily invested in solar and wind power to make itself energy sufficient [25]. Besides that, Dell ensures the manufacture of products that are energy sufficient in line with environmental standards. Almost half of the energy used by Dell is from green sources, about 225,000,000 kWh per annum [25].

Google cannot be left behind in the use of green energy on the account that they are one of the biggest advocates for green energy. Since 2007, Google has been carbon neutral and it utilities a total of approximately 735,000,000 kWh of green energy per year. Most of the energy is used to power its data centers as it is more reliable than the traditional power grid systems [25]. Google is also consistently researching novel ways of tapping and utilizing green energy in enhancing sustainability and operational efficiency for industries that are heavily dependent on intensive power use [25].

IBM has been one of the 'green' leaders in tech for a number of years, dating back to 1967 when it issued its first policy on environmental affairs. Big Blue states on its website that they will: "Use development and manufacturing processes that do not adversely affect the environment, including developing and improving operations and technologies to minimize waste, prevent air, water, and other pollution, minimize health and safety risks, and dispose of waste safely and responsibly." The company is very open about its achievements and failings when it comes to its environmental policy, for example detailing its hazardous waste performances [25].

Cisco has been working hard to meet targets on Greenhouse gasses, which it met in 2012 and is now working work to reduce them further. The company has in the past year built 3 solar photovoltaic systems in Texas and Bangalore, which will produce 2 million kilowatt hours of electricity annually and save over $380,000. They also help to prevent more than 1150 metric ton of carbon emissions each year [25]. Cisco Systems is a tech company increasingly exploring the use of green energy to ramp up its operations and support its power demands. It works towards doubling its green energy use by the end of the 2021 fiscal year. Cisco Systems' motive is to prove to the world that green energy plays a critical role in creating a sustainable power use strategy across the entire IT industry. Its primary target is to reduce greenhouse gas emissions and embrace a greener business outlook. Cisco has built into its products, solutions which aim to reduce energy use such as EnergyWise and JouleX, which reduce energy consumption in commercial and residential buildings [25].

Microsoft qualifies as the greenest technology company in the world. This is an attribute given to Microsoft cooperation because it utilizes more than 1.3 billion kWh of green energy on an annual basis. Microsoft works day in and out to ascertain its electric power requirements are supported by green energy [25]. Microsoft is also sufficiently carbon neutral as the green energy is sourced from solar and wind power with the most sustainable mechanisms. The green energy is used to power Microsoft's data centers, software development facilities, and in product manufacturing [25].

Sprint's commitment to reduce greenhouse gas emission by 20% is the reason it has embraced the use of green power. The plan has made Sprint indulge in the use of on-site clean energy to power and facilitate the operations of its energy-hungry facilities [25]. Sprint has also partnered with clean energy research firms in a bid to seek better ways of investing in clean energy and back-up power within the site. The clean energy sources used by Sprint include wind and solar power which has been perfected by the installation of wind turbines and solar panels [25].

HP (Hewlett Packard) as one of the world's top tech companies is as well not left behind when it comes to the exploitation of green energy. The enterprise powers about 20% of its technology and services in helping customers around the globe to become more IT efficient by the use of green energy. Also, the company has recently come up with a goal of sourcing more than 40% of its cumulative energy consumption from clean energy sources by 2020, and 100% clean energy in the long-term [25-30].

Sony utilizes green energy by predominantly purchasing its power requirements from renewable energy sources. The green energy it purchases is about 88,000,000 kWh which caters to approximately 37% of its yearly energy consumption. This is quite commendable considering the size of the company. The company's drive to using green energy is influenced by its commitment to minimizing its negative environmental impacts and greenhouse gas emissions. Sony believes environmental sustainability is partly achievable by increasing the percentage of renewable energy powering a company's operations and services [25-30].

SAP is a global leader in the provision of software and its related services. The company has a dedicated branch supporting the use of renewable energy and is devoted to sustainable practices in its operations, designs, and manufacturing. The amount of green energy used annually by the company totals to about 86,000,000 kWh [25-30].

For instance, the company came up with a goal to buy over 350 gigawatt-hours of green energy across the world to power its data centers. At the same time, the company promises to have a neutral carbon footprint.

In the latest reaction from the whole world for the application of GIT can be seen in the world submit started on NOV 1 202112:53, where world leaders are promising actions to preserve the environment and stressing on the applications of GIT for all the levels of BPO. Future work will explain the results of the actions planned by the world leaders.

Conclusion

For past few decades IT has secured an important place and all disciplines are using IT for its better performances. BPO has also been using IT for its all operations for increasing productivity and other important results but in the due time IT has also increased a major concern of environment pollution and threat to flora, fauna and to human lives in general. Therefore, it was important to reduce the applications of IT for BPO or look for other options to preserve the environment. GIT gave the options to all firms in all types of BPO to follow eco-friendly options and aid in preventing the increase in pollutions. Although GIT may increase cost but in the long run firms will achieve profit and just like examples given in the results section other firms can follow their foot prints and become the benchmark for other firms. This paper suggests all BPO to use GIT and support GIT in all government sectors and business operations, publish awareness among citizens and businesses about the importance of GIT. BPO can use GIT for all levels by using computers like thin client that reduces energy consumption, cooperation with specialized companies to get rid of unwanted computers and make a safe disposal or recycling. GIT is not an option for BPO in the current situation rather a need and protocol to be followed.

References

[1] Airehrour, D., Cherrington, M., Madanian, S., & Singh, J. (2019, August). Reducing ICT carbon footprints through adoption of green computing. In *10.12948/ie2019. 04.17*. Academy of Economic Studies in Bucharest. Department of Economic Informatics and Cybernetics.

[2] Mohapatra, S. K., Nayak, P., Mishra, S., & Bisoy, S. K. (2019). Green computing: a step towards eco-friendly computing. In *Emerging trends and applications in cognitive computing* (pp. 124-149). IGI Global.

[3] Naim, A. (2018). Strategies to Achieve Students' Centric Approach in Blended Learning. *International Journal of Engineering and Management Research (IJEMR)*, 8(2), 214-219.

[4] Herath, H. S., Herath, T. C., & Dunn, P. (2019). Profit-driven corporate social responsibility as a Bayesian real option in green computing. *Journal of Business Ethics*, *158*(2), 387-402.

[5] Naim, A., Hussain, M. R., Naveed, Q. N., Ahmad, N., Qamar, S., Khan, N., & Hweij, T. A. (2019, April). Ensuring interoperability of e-learning and quality development in education. In *2019 IEEE Jordan International Joint Conference on Electrical Engineering and Information Technology (JEEIT)* (pp. 736-741). IEEE.

[6] Ojo, A. O., Raman, M., & Downe, A. G. (2019). Toward green computing practices: A Malaysian study of green belief and attitude among

Information Technology professionals. *Journal of cleaner production, 224*, 246-255.

[7] Singh, G., & Mahajan, M. (2019). A green computing supportive allocation scheme utilizing genetic algorithm and support vector machine. *Computing*, *23*, 24.

[8] Naim, A., Khan, M. F., Hussain, M. R., & Khan, N. (2019). "Virtual Doctor" Management Technique in the Diagnosis of ENT Diseases. *JOE*, *15*(9), 88.

[9] Mihai, C. I. O. C., & URSĂCESCU, M. (2019). The State Of It Human Resources about the Capabilities of Adopting Green Computing Practices: A Romanian Perspective. In *Proceedings of the International Management Conference* (Vol. 13, No. 1, pp. 856-862). Faculty of Management, Academy of Economic Studies, Bucharest, Romania.

[10] Naim, A., & Alahmari, F. (2020). Reference model of e-learning and quality to establish interoperability in higher education systems. *International Journal of Emerging Technologies in Learning (iJET),* 15(2), 15-28.

[11] Jayalath, J. M. T. I., Chathumali, E. J. A. P. C., Kothalawala, K. R. M., & Kuruwitaarachchi, N. (2019, March). Green cloud computing: A review on adoption of green-computing attributes and vendor specific implementations. In *2019 International Research Conference on Smart Computing and Systems Engineering (SCSE)* (pp. 158-164). IEEE.

[12] Bindhu, V., & Joe, M. (2019). Green cloud computing solution for operational cost efficiency and environmental impact reduction. *Journal of ISMAC*, *1*(02), 120-128.

[13] Naim, A. (2020). Realization of diverse Electronic tools in learning and teaching for students with diverse skills. *Global Journal of Enterprise Information System,* 12(1), 72-78.

[14] Khan, S. N., Aljaberi, M. A., & Muammar, S. (2019). Success factors model for green computing implementations. *International Journal of Technology Management & Sustainable Development,* 18(1), 37-54.

[15] Botchway, S. D. R., & Sheela, L. M. I. (2019). A study on destructive environment impacts on green computing. *Advance and Innovative Research*, 364.

[16] Naim, A., & Bashir, A. (2016). Application of Quality Matters Standards on Supportive and Online Module in Higher Education Program. *Research Revolution*, 5(3), 6-12.

[17] Mohapatra, S. K., Nayak, P., Mishra, S., & Bisoy, S. K. (2019). Green computing: a step towards eco-friendly computing. In *Emerging trends and applications in cognitive computing* (pp. 124-149). IGI Global.

[18] Patil, A., & Patil, D. (2019, February). An Analysis Report on Green Cloud Computing Current Trends and Future Research Challenges. In

Proceedings of International Conference on Sustainable Computing in Science, Technology and Management (SUSCOM), Amity University Rajasthan, Jaipur-India.

[19] Naim, A., Sattar, R. A., Al Ahmary, N., & Razwi, M. T. (2021) *Implementation of Quality Matters Standards on Blended Courses: A Case Study*. FINANCE INDIA Indian Institute of Finance Vol. XXXV No. 3, September 2021 Pages—873 – 890.

[20] Sengupta, G. (2019). Green Computing–New Perspective of Efficient Usage of Energy and Reduction of E-Waste. *Journal of Technology and Innovation in Tertiary Education*, 2(1), 11-16.

[21] Scionti, A., Terzo, O., Ruiu, P., Giordanengo, G., Ciccia, S., Urlini, G., & Harryvan, D. (2019). The Green Computing Continuum: The OPERA Perspective. In *Hardware Accelerators in Data Centers* (pp. 57-86). Springer, Cham.

[22] Kaur, M. A., & Kaur, M. S. (2019). *Green Computing: Emerging* Issues in IT.

[23] Herath, H. S., Herath, T. C., & Dunn, P. (2019). Profit-driven corporate social responsibility as a Bayesian real option in green computing. *Journal of Business Ethics*, 158(2), 387-402.

[24] Bindhu, V., & Joe, M. (2019). Green cloud computing solution for operational cost efficiency and environmental impact reduction. *Journal of ISMAC*, 1(02), 120-128.

[25] Franca, R. P., Iano, Y., Monteiro, A. C. B., & Arthur, R. (2021). Better Transmission of Information Focused on Green Computing Through Data Transmission Channels in Cloud Environments with Rayleigh Fading. In *Green Computing in Smart Cities: Simulation and Techniques* (pp. 71-93). Springer, Cham.

[26] Naim, A. (2021). Application of Quality Matters in Digital Learning in Higher Education. *Texas Journal of Multidisciplinary* Studies, 1(1), 3-12.

[27] Okewu, E., Misra, S., Maskeliūnas, R., Damaševičius, R., & Fernandez-Sanz, L. (2017). Optimizing green computing awareness for environmental sustainability and economic security as a stochastic optimization problem. *Sustainability*, 9(10), 1857.

[28] Naim, A., Alahmari, F., & Rahim, A. (2021). Role of Artificial Intelligence in Market Development and Vehicular Communication. *Smart Antennas: Recent Trends in Design and Applications,* 2, 28.

[29] Irimiás, A., & Mitev, A. (2020). Change Management, Digital Maturity, and Green Development: Are Successful Firms Leveraging on Sustainability? *Sustainability,* 12(10), 4019.

Chapter 4

Consumer Behavior Appraisal for Health and Fitness Services

Arshi Naim[1,*] and Mohammad Faiz Khan[2,†]
[1]Department of Information Systems,
King Khalid University, Abha, Kingdom of Saudi Arabia (KSA)
[2]Security Forces Hospital, Abha, Kingdom of Saudi Arabia (KSA)

Abstract

The objective of the research is to understand Psychographic aspect of Consumer Behavior for health services which can lead to develop proactive purchase behavior for fitness and health products. Data was collected from primary sources that include Medical Practitioners, Medical Representatives and Patients. Research method is adaptive in this study as it tries to influence present psychographic consumer behavior towards health and fitness. To measure responses of consumers, we have used likert scale. Both Qualitative and Quantitative research methods are used to evaluate optimal health solutions and financial outcomes for fitness and health services. Responses collected through primary data are represented in the form of tables and graph for conclusive and descriptive findings. Consumers confidently choose products and aspire to have best value for the money but when it comes to choosing medicines and care, they are often found to be confused. This study also gives recommendations to some Consumer organizations such as Consumers Union and Medical Organization to design program or

* Corresponding Author's Email: arshi@kku.edu.sa.
† Corresponding Author's Email: mfaizkhan@hotmail.com.

In: Competitive Trends and Technologies in Business Management
Editors: Arshi Naim and Praveen K. Malik
ISBN: 978-1-68507-612-2

medical aid campaigns to help consumer's select best options for medical services and can acquire information about medical care as well as financial solutions for fitness and health issues. This research has contributed in two ways, one to know consumer behavior for health services that can help medical service providers to develop effective communication programs and secondly consumer awareness regarding medical care and financial aid.

Keywords: consumer behavior, psychographic, optimal health, financial outcome

1. Introduction

Under Social utility health centers have to know Psychographic aspects which include Consumer's Motive, Need, Learning, Perception and attitude which however can bring proactive behavior for understanding health's significance and as an outcome our society can move to achieve better health [1]. Under commercial utility, health centers can learn better communication program which can direct consumers towards them as well as they can know the market of medical aid. Health centers have to know the demographic which too is responsible to establish a kind of consumer behavior as it is affected by age, income level, education, and living standard. Demographic evaluation will not only result in defining consumer age and income level but also consumer purchase behavior which is based on convenience of location [1]. Therefore this research will bring observatory report for commercial act for the health centers to create awareness of wellbeing and can derive optimum revenue too. Figure 1 shows the list of concepts that have been used to elaborate the purpose of the study:

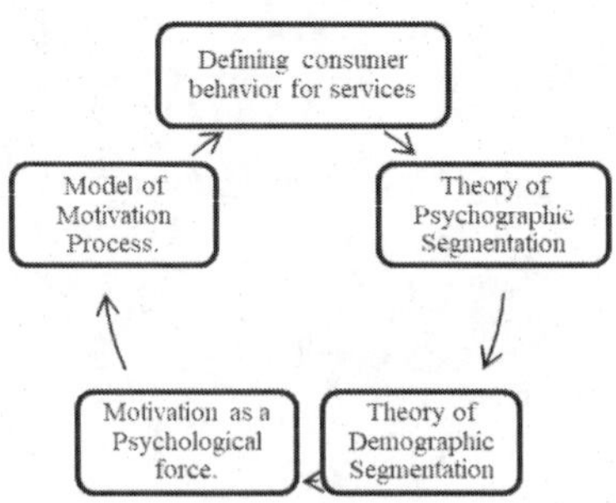

Figure 1. Theoritical concepts of the study [1].

1.1. Purpose of the Study

The objective of the research is to understand Psychographic aspect of Consumer Behavior for health services and accordingly effort to understand how proactive behavior can be inculcated amongst consumers for health and fitness. This research will deal with trivial health issues which when not cared due to kind of behavior give serious outcome, however, this study will also help medical service providers to know consumer behavior for their service thereafter they can also get an aid to design communication Strategy [1, 2]. Rising standard of living has brought about development in the personal care services helping a customer to be well groomed. These services are offered by the health care and fitness centers. For the purpose of this study to define CB for health services consumer behavior will be known under following criterion shown in Figure 2.

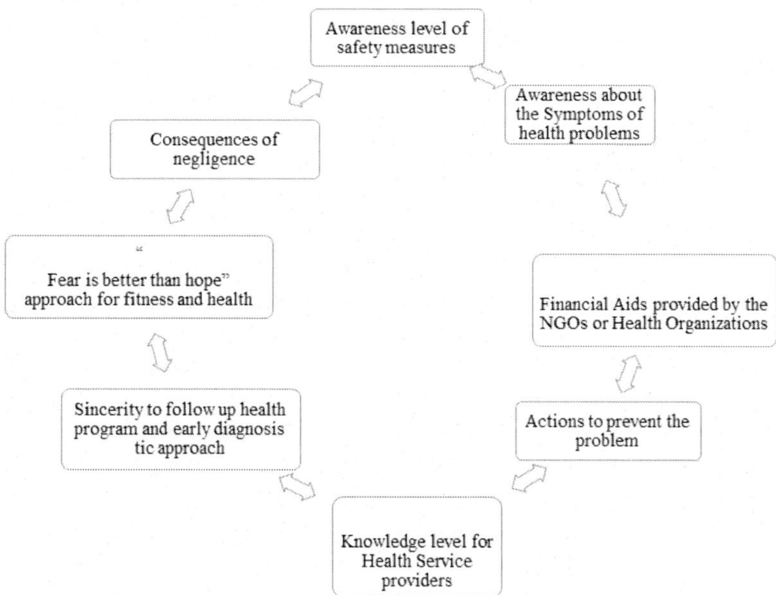

Figure 2. Concepts of consumer behavior for health services [1, 2].

1.2. Scope of the Study

The approach of this study will help health centers to understand CB for health services so that they can earn social as well commercial utility.

Under Social utility Health centers have to know Psychographic aspects which include Consumer's Motive, Need, Learning, Perception and attitude which however can bring proactive behavior for understanding health's significance and as an outcome our society can move to achieve better health.

Under commercial utility, health centers can learn better communication program which can direct consumers towards them as well as they can know the market of medical aid.

Also health centers have to know the demographic which too is responsible to establish a kind of consumer behavior as it is affected by age, income level, education, and living standard. Demographic evaluation will not only result in defining consumer's age, income level but also consumer purchase behavior which is based on convenience of location. Therefore this research will bring observatory report for commercial act for the health centers to create awareness of wellbeing and can derive optimum revenue too.

2. Literature Review

American Academy of Dermatology identifies Organization Behavior as "US trends in lifestyles are a shift towards personal independence and individualism and a preference for a healthy, natural lifestyle" and to achieve this individual join specialty clinics such as skin care clinics and make regular visit to dietician. Lifestyles are the consistent patterns people follow in their lives. For example "Healthy and Balanced Food for a Healthy Lifestyle" is recommended.

CVS Caremark Corp talks in almost every sector of the economy, consumers confidently choose products that provide the best value for the money. But when it comes to choosing medicines, they often find themselves adrift amid confusing products, marketing claims and opaque pricing points, a situation that doesn't always lead to the best or certainly the least expensive therapies. Consumer organizations such as Consumers Union are designing programs to help consumers select options that will provide optimal health and financial outcomes. Consumers have a need for impartial information about their drug options, John Santa, MD, director of the Health Rating Center for Consumer Reports Health, said at a press conference on Capitol Hill on March 17 [2].

Thomson Reuters analyzed consumer data from the PULSE Healthcare Survey. The study has nine waves covering more than 80 healthcare topics, including health status, Psychology of consumer for fitness and health, insurance coverage, physician and ambulatory care services, hospital inpatient services, health behaviors and attitudes, current healthcare topics and issues. This study focuses on PULSE consumer data collected between January 2006 and February 2009. Ann Arbor, MI April 20, 2009 – Psychology of consumer for health and fitness defines delays and cancel behavior for following health reasons.

Thomson Reuters study finds more patients postponing medical care due to cost. Science Daily identifies consumer behavior for health services in Indian context in lower public strata and defines ways to provide and communicate lower public costs for social services by improving children's long term welfare, such as pulse polio program, measures against weight loss amongst children, and malnutrition, etc.

Table 1. Reasons for delays for fitness and health [2]

Reasons for delays in diagnosis and treatment
Delay or cancel healthcare treatment for a child under the age of 15.
Delay or cancel therapy such as physical therapy, rehabilitation therapy, and respiratory therapy.
Delay or cancel an elective surgical procedure such as LASIK eye surgery or plastic/cosmetic surgery.
Delay or cancel a diagnostic test such as blood work, x-ray, mammogram, etc.
Delay or cancel a doctor visit for treating a minor illness or injury such as flu, earache, sprained ankle.
Delay or cancel a routine doctor visit such as an annual physical

Journal of Science Daily talks of the latest research on what motivates people to buy, how brand names affect the brain, fitness, gene therapy, and heart disease [2]. Journal of Science Daily mentioned that the fear of looking unattractive can be a stronger motivation for keeping people going to the gym than the hope of racial issues in perception in consumer behavior. Info Shop study says, "Active consumer is alive," well, and affluent and spending money on fitness-related service, this section of the report analyzes the consumer behavior of fit consumers. Sb information explains buying resistance problem begins with understanding how consumers or companies make buying decisions in free educational fitness seminar.

US Penguin Group develops an intuitive understanding of consumer behavior and marketing strategies to flaunt and fake their biological fitness under the prospects for survival [2, 3]. Scrib Indian Consumer outlook talks about fitness amongst youth in India, and the psychological characteristics in the context of Indian consumer behavior which is "Service quality is fitness for use [2, 3].

3. Discussion

3.1. Details of Hypothesis

Detail definition of the terms through secondary data and understanding stipulations under health services has been accounted. Consumer psychology is the study of the dynamics underlying consumer behavior specifically concentrating on the use of psychological concepts and methods to explain predict and influence behavior (Assail, 1992). Table 2 presents the four consumer psychological models used for this study.

Table 2. List of consumer psychological models [3-6]

Learning Model
The Dynamics of Motivation: Types and Systems of Need- Maslow's Need Hierarchy
Personality and Consumer Behavior: Brand Personality and Understand Consumer Diversity and Consumer Imagery.
Consumer Learning For Services and Behavioral Learning Theories

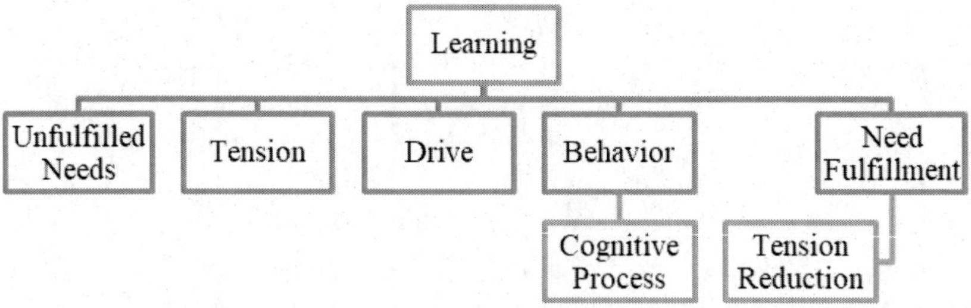

Figure 3. Learning model of consumer psychology [3-6].

Figure 4 shows the Dynamics of Motivation as the types and systems of need explained by Maslow's Need Hierarchy theory and this is the second hypothesis for consumer psychology that we have applied.

Figure 4. Maslow's need hierarchy [3-6].

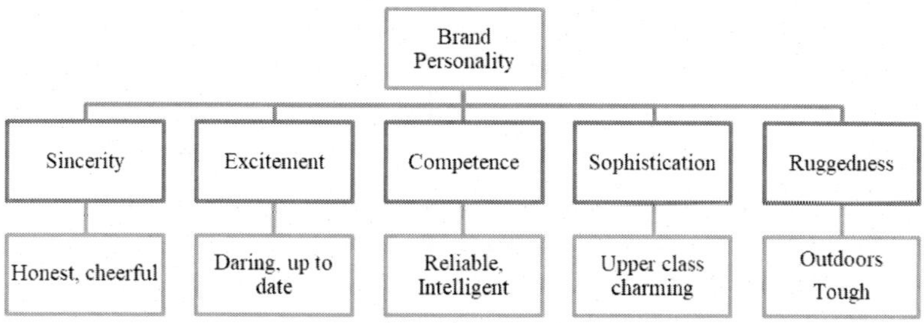

Figure 5. Personality and Consumer Behavior: Brand Personality and Understand Consumer Diversity and Consumer Imagery [3-6].

Table 3. Consumer learning for services and behavioral learning theories [3-6]

Promotional Model	**Tri component Model**	**Decision making Model**	**Innovation Adoption Model**	**Innovation Decision Process**
Attention	Cognitive	Awareness Knowledge	Awareness	Knowledge
Interest Desire	Affective	Evaluation	Interest Evaluation	Persuasion
Action	Cognitive	Purchase Post purchase evaluation	Trial Adoption	Decision Confirmation

3.2. Research Methodology

Since the research is descriptive in nature, Qualitative approach is applied for results evaluation. Research methodology is systematic gathering, recording and analyzing of data about the Psychological approach to consumer behavior for health services.

The research has following scope [4]:

a. Planning
b. Interpreting

The study design consisted of taking a cross-sectional view from both stakeholders– doctors and patients about healthcare delivery and utilization.

The medium used was a questionnaire designed on the Likert scale and Servqual 5 dimensions were considered for designing the questions. The questionnaire was administered via internet and telephonic interview. For the purpose of this study 25 direct consumers (patients) and 50 persons related to the consumers were interviewed.

25 healthcare providers were included in the study.

3.3. Research Design

There can be many types of research design but broadly there are three [4]:

a. Descriptive
b. Experimental
c. Quasi- Experimental

Research design for this study was Descriptive as descriptive design describes phenomenon without establishing association between factors such as behavioral variables and situational variables. Therefore, the study demands for descriptive research design which was intended to produce accurate descriptions of variable relevant to the decisions, without demonstrating the relationship between the variables.

Perception measurement was done through Servqual Scale which measured the gap between Customer expectations of services and their perception of actual services.

This scale is based on 5 dimensions-Reliability, Responsiveness, Assurance, Empathy and Tangibility. Further Likert Scale was used to scale the respondent from extreme range like strongly agree to strongly disagree.

Data types are nearly innumerable which can be obtained according to the nature of study which is given in the Figure 4.

In this study demographic and psychographic factors are used in particular and following aspects were covered. Table 4 and 5 show the factors covered in both segmentations.

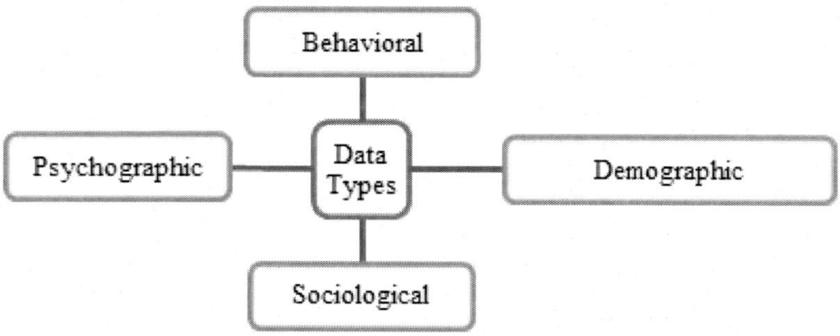

Figure 6. Data types for consumer behavior [4, 5].

Table 4. Demographic segmentation [4]

Gender
Marital Status
Age
Educational Level
Occupation
Income Level

Table 5. Psychological segmentation [5]

Knowledge
Opinions
Intentions
Motives

3.4. Consumer Research Process

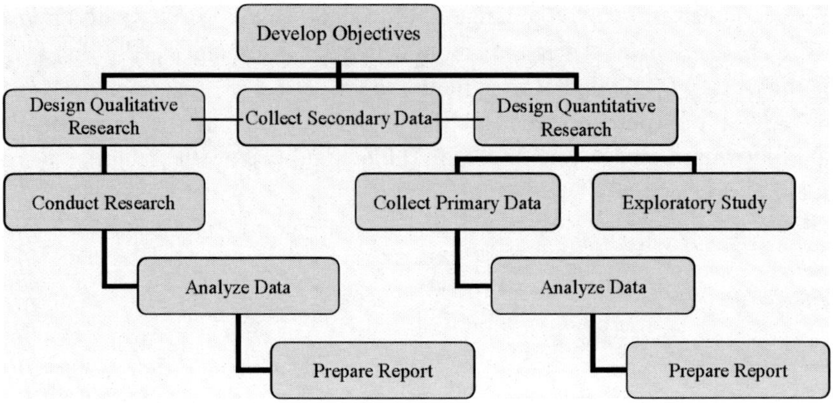

Figure 7. Consumer research process [4, 5].

3.5. Data Types

We have used primary as well as secondary data to file results. The Primary data was collected from primary source which were Medical Practitioners, Medical Representatives and Patients. Research method was adaptive as it tried to influence present psychographic consumer behavior towards health and fitness and for measuring responses likert scale was used. To evaluate optimal health and financial outcomes for fitness, Qualitative research method was used. Both structured and unstructured questionnaires were used for primary data collection and results are represented in the form of tables and graph to show the conclusive and descriptive findings. The data was collected according to following categories shown in the Figure 8.

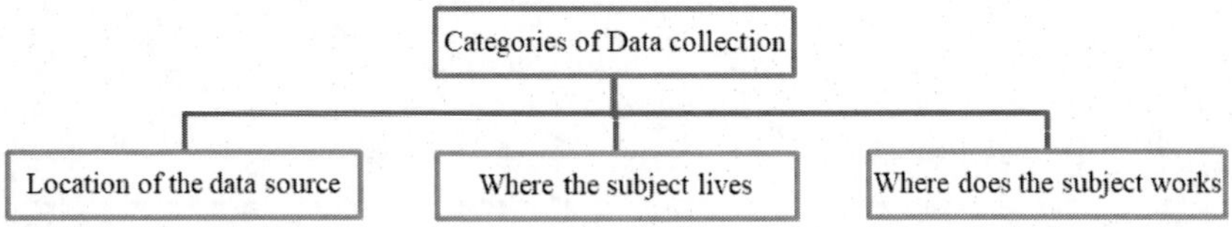

Figure 8. Data category [5-7].

For the purpose of this study following media was used to collect data and Figure 9 shows the list of media.

Questions were both close and open ended as research object was descriptive. Secondary Data is collected from consumer behavior's books for services, journal, periodical, newsletters, and magazines.

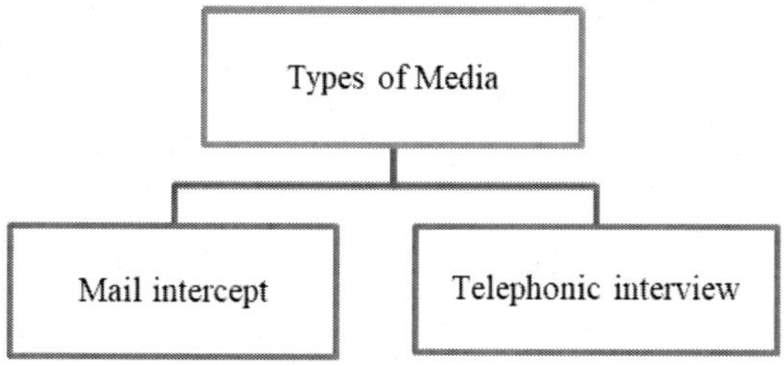

Figure 9. Media Selection and Communication Approaches [6, 7].

3.6. Scaling Method for This Study

For the purpose of demographic information six different close ended questions were asked and for detailed information five open ended questions were asked which gave a chance to the respondents to explain their opinions and awareness on fitness issue.

For measuring Consumer perception and expectation for service quality for health care and fitness Servqual 5 dimensions were measured for 21 Questions which were closed ended, 5 points likert scale ranging from Strongly Disagree to Strongly Agree was used for investigating results.

Perception was measured through Servqual Scale; this measured the gap between Customer expectations of services and their perception of actual services. This scale is based on 5 Dimensions-Reliability, Responsiveness, Assurance, Empathy and Tangibility.

Table 6 shows the dimensions and statements measured by Servqual Dimensions in Likert Scale.

Table 6. Dimensions of Measurement

Dimension	Statements Pertaining to Dimension
Tangible	1-4
Reliability	5-8
Responsiveness	9- 12
Assurance	13-16
Empathy	17-21

There are many factors that can influence desired and predictive Medical services for consumers, these factors are shown in Figure 10 [7-9].

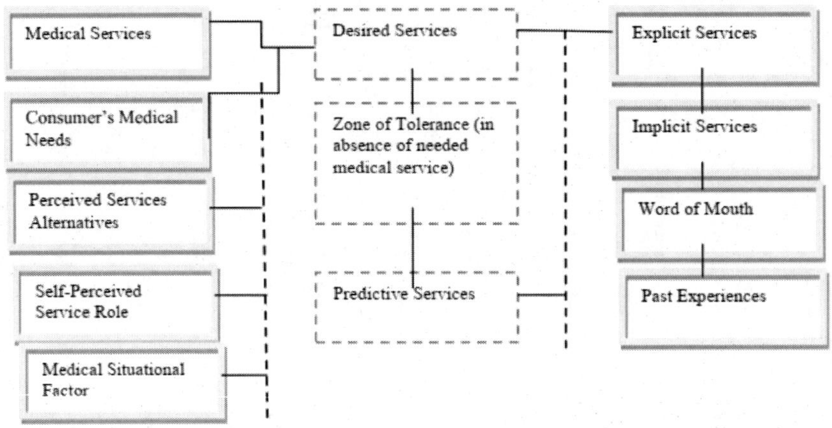

Figure 10. Factors for medical services for consumers [7-9].

Table 7. Questionnaire for demographic information

Please Specify your Gender	Male	Female		
Please specify your marital status	Single	Married		
Please indicate your age category	Below 24	25-34	35-45	45 and above
What is your highest level of qualification	Intermediate	Graduation	PG	Doctorate
Please specify your monthly income level	<10000	<15000	<200000	<50000
What is your occupation	Doctor	Teacher	Entrepreneur	Others

Table 8. Open ended psychological questionnaire

Do you think health related issues are concern of security need and should be dealt urgently? For Yes or No Give reasons for your answer.
Why do you think it's important to receive treatment in specialized health care centers?
What are the motivating features you look for in health care centers?
What kind of health awareness program you think is the best from health care organization to inform on important issues related to fitness and health?
What is the best media for health awareness program that health care organization can opt for and why?

Table 9. Questions that measured psychological particulars [10, 11]

Factors	Related Query	Expected level Strongly Disagree Strongly Agree							Actually Received Strongly Disagree - Strongly Agree						
Tangible	Excellent Health Care Centers have Modern investigating machine.	1	2	3	4	5	6	7	1	2	3	4	5	6	7
	Physical Amenities of health care are excellent and appealing to consumer mindset.	1	2	3	4	5	6	7	1	2	3	4	5	6	7
	Medical Staff is neat and good in appearance.	1	2	3	4	5	6	7	1	2	3	4	5	6	7
	Equipment associated to the service such as cardio and weight training equipment	1	2	3	4	5	6	7	1	2	3	4	5	6	7
Reliability	Excellent Health Care org provide membership that makes medical facility easy and cheaper to purchase.	1	2	3	4	5	6	7	1	2	3	4	5	6	7
	Medical Staff are responsive to customers complaints	1	2	3	4	5	6	7	1	2	3	4	5	6	7
	Medical Staff are prepared for Emergencies	1	2	3	4	5	6	7	1	2	3	4	5	6	7
	Health Care Org Offer prompt service to its members	1	2	3	4	5	6	7	1	2	3	4	5	6	7
Responsiveness	Medical Staff offer exact consultation to the customers as per their health related need.	1	2	3	4	5	6	7	1	2	3	4	5	6	7
	Child Minders in excellent health care interact and play with children as a part of Health Care USP	1	2	3	4	5	6	7	1	2	3	4	5	6	7
	Medical Staff are always willing to help	1	2	3	4	5	6	7	1	2	3	4	5	6	7
	Medical Staff are professions and trained while dealing health related issues.	1	2	3	4	5	6	7	1	2	3	4	5	6	7
Assurance	Medical Staff instill confidence in consumers.	1	2	3	4	5	6	7	1	2	3	4	5	6	7
	Medical Centers provide secure and safe facilities to consumers	1	2	3	4	5	6	7	1	2	3	4	5	6	7
	As a part to offer concession to Health care members offer moderate membership fees.	1	2	3	4	5	6	7	1	2	3	4	5	6	7
	Medical Staff Have Professional Knowledge	1	2	3	4	5	6	7	1	2	3	4	5	6	7
Empathy	Medical Staff show interest in consumer's improvement	1	2	3	4	5	6	7	1	2	3	4	5	6	7
	Medical Staff give individual attention	1	2	3	4	5	6	7	1	2	3	4	5	6	7
	Health Care Org provide members social opportunity as part of Medical USP	1	2	3	4	5	6	7	1	2	3	4	5	6	7
	Medical Staff Understands the specific needs of all consumers	1	2	3	4	5	6	7	1	2	3	4	5	6	7
	Health Care center have 24 hrs operating services.	1	2	3	4	5	6	7	1	2	3	4	5	6	7

Table 7 shows the list of questions pertaining to personal information where consumers were asked to cross or tick to present their data for their demographic profile.

Some Open ended questions were also asked to analyze psychological behavior of consumers; Table 8 shows the list of questions.

For the purpose of the study closed ended questions were also asked from the consumers for psychological behavior for fitness and health. Consumers were asked to answer questions for five factors such as tangibility, Reliability, Responsiveness, Assurance and Empathy under psychological behavior, Table 9 shows the questions on all these factors [10, 11]. Consumers were asked to rate on 7 scale from strongly disagree to strongly agree for measuring expected value and real value for all the five factors.

4. Results

4.1. Demographic Findings

Figures 9 to 13 show the demographic results, this information was important to understand the profile of consumers and then to analyze their psychological response to health and fitness. Our respondents were more from female groups and they were found extra careful for their fitness than of other medical related issues and they were found spending on keeping fitness plan.

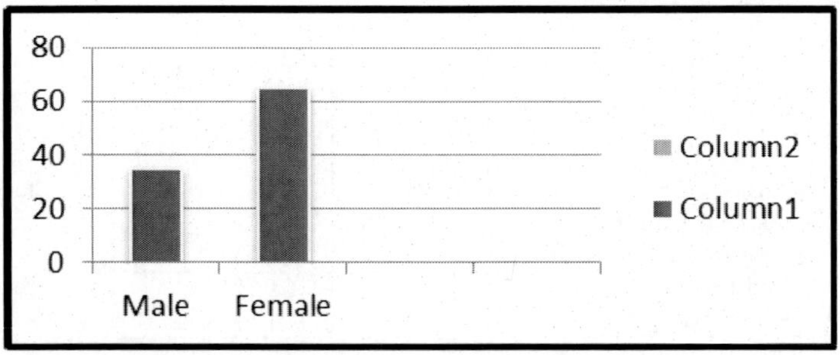

Figure 9. Gender information.

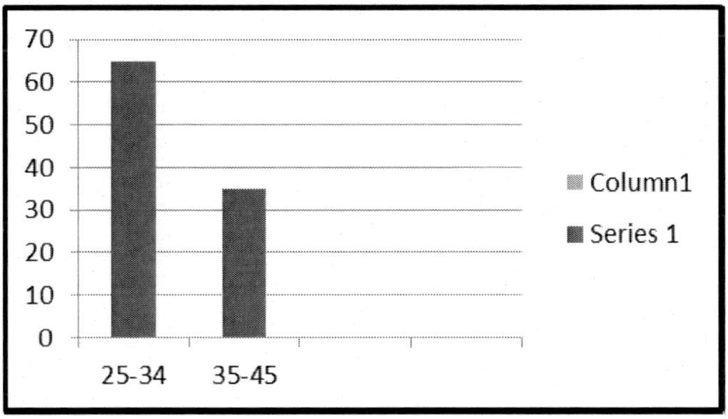

Figure 10. Age category.

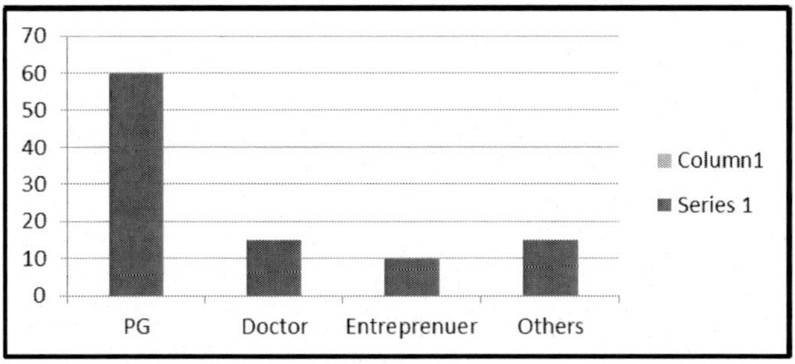

Figure 11. Level of Education.

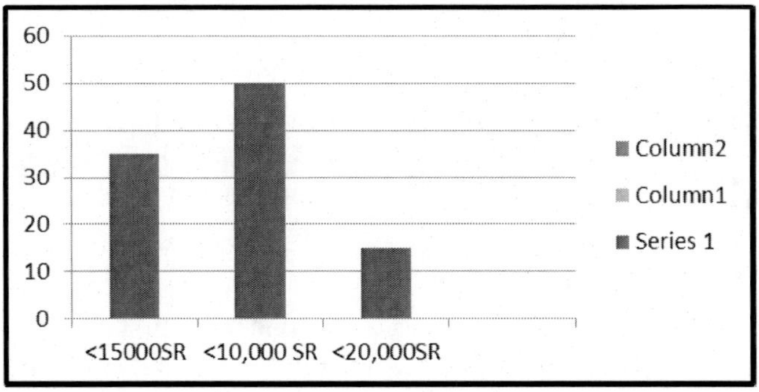

Figure 12. Monthly Income.

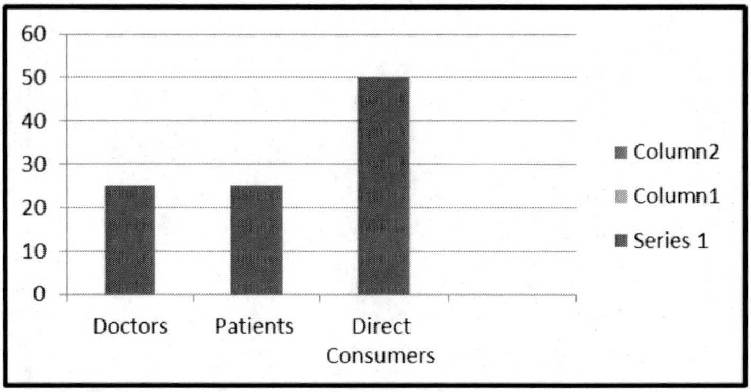

Figure 13. Occupation.

Young age groups show good response to fitness and medical services than of middle aged groups.

Usually it is assumed that people from educated class and good income groups will not delay the health related issues and give extra care to their fitness. One strange result was noticed that groups from social science or academics were found to be using more of fitness and medical services than of medical professionals. The reasons for these results were not known and as a result are not described in this chapter.

4.2. Psychological Finding

4.2.1. Tangibility

Expected level was very high as most of respondents choose 7 degree on likert scale but Actual received services were moderate as most respondents choose from 4 to 6 degree on likert scale.

4.2.2. Reliability

Expected level was very high as most of respondents choose 7 degree on likert scale but Actual received services were less than moderate as most respondents choose from 3 to 5 degree on likert scale.

4.2.3. Responsiveness

Expected level was very high as most of respondents choose 7 degree but few respondents choose lowest degree too such as 2 on likert scale but Actual received services were less than moderate as most respondents choose from 3 to 6 degree on likert scale.

4.2.4. Assurance

Expected level was very high as most of respondents choose 7 degree likert scale but Actual received services were poor as most respondents choose from 1 to 4 degree on likert scale.

4.2.5. Empathy

Expected level was very high as most of respondents choose 7 degree likert scale but Actual received services were from poor to moderate as respondents choose from 1 to 6 degree on likert scale.

Consumers confidently choose products that provide the best value for the money. When it comes to choosing medicines and care, they often find themselves confused due to lack of information. Consumer organizations such as Consumers Union, Medical Organization can design program or medical aid campaign to help consumers select options that will provide optimal health and financial outcomes to fitness and health care. Also Consumers can have information about medical care as well as financial solutions to acquire fitness and health care through Consumer union and Medical organization.

The results indicated that the service quality dimensions predicted significant and high proportions of variances in word-of-mouth communications and purchase intentions across all three facilities. The tangible and assurance dimensions offered the most significant contributions. The results further revealed no significant relationships between the price sensitivity and complaining behavior dimensions and perceptions of service quality. These results have theoretical implications for developing a framework for conceptualizing service loyalty and identifying its antecedents. They also have practical implications for designing effective customer retention strategies.

Conclusion

This research has contributed in two ways one to know consumer behavior for health services for medical service providers so that they can make communication program and secondly consumer awareness regarding medical care as and financial aid.

References

[1] Švecová, J., & Odehnalová, P. (2019). The determinants of consumer behaviour of students from Brno when purchasing organic food. *Review of Economic Perspectives*, *19*(1), 49-64.

[2] Ting, C. Y., Ismail, M. B., Ting, H., Bahri, S. B., Sidek, A. B., Idris, S. F. B., ... & Sohot, M. S. B. (2019). Consumer behaviour towards pharmaceutical products: A model development. *International Journal of Pharmaceutical and Healthcare Marketing*.

[3] Naim, A. (2021). Application of Quality Matters in Digital Learning in Higher Education. *Texas Journal of Multidisciplinary Studies*, *1*(1), 3-12.

[4] Pham, T. H., Nguyen, T. N., Phan, T. T. H., & Nguyen, N. T. (2019). Evaluating the purchase behaviour of organic food by young consumers in an emerging market economy. *Journal of Strategic Marketing*, *27*(6), 540-556.

[5] Khan, N., Naim, A., Hussain, M. R., Naveed, Q. N., Ahmad, N., & Qamar, S. (2019, May). The 51 v's of big data: survey, technologies, characteristics, opportunities, issues and challenges. In *Proceedings of the international conference on omni-layer intelligent systems* (pp. 19-24).

[6] Naim, A. (2020). Realization of diverse Electronic tools in learning and teaching for students with diverse skills. *Global Journal of Enterprise Information System*, *12*(1), 72-78.

[7] Weinrich, R. (2019). Opportunities for the adoption of health-based sustainable dietary patterns: A review on consumer research of meat substitutes. *Sustainability*, *11*(15), 4028.

[8] Aschwanden, D., Strickhouser, J. E., Sesker, A. A., Lee, J. H., Luchetti, M., Stephan, Y., ... & Terracciano, A. (2021). Psychological and behavioural responses to coronavirus disease 2019: The role of personality. *European Journal of Personality*, *35*(1), 51-66.

[9] Naim, A., & Alahmari, F. (2020). Reference model of e-learning and quality to establish interoperability in higher education systems. *International Journal of Emerging Technologies in Learning (iJET)*, *15*(2), 15-28.

[10] Joshi, Y., & Rahman, Z. (2019). Consumers' sustainable purchase behaviour: Modeling the impact of psychological factors. *Ecological economics*, *159*, 235-243.

[11] Gonçalves, C., Meireles, P., & Carvalho, M. J. (2016). Consumer behaviour in Fitness Club: study of the weekly frequency of use, expectations, satisfaction and retention. *The Open Sports Sciences Journal*, *9*(1).

[12] Naim, A., Khan, M. F., Hussain, M. R., & Khan, N. (2019). "Virtual Doctor" Management Technique in the Diagnosis of ENT Diseases. *JOE*, *15*(9), 88.

[13] Qalati, S., Yuan, L., Iqbal, S., Hussain, R., & Ali, S. (2019). Impact of Price on Customer Satisfaction; mediating role of Consumer Buying Behaviour in Telecom Sector. *International Journal of Research*, *6*(4), 150-165.

[14] Qazzafi, S. H. E. I. K. H. (2019). Consumer buying decision process toward products. International Journal of Scientific Research and Engineering Development, 2(5), 130-134.

[15] Naim, A., Hussain, M. R., Naveed, Q. N., Ahmad, N., Qamar, S., Khan, N., & Hweij, T. A. (2019, April). Ensuring interoperability of e-learning and quality development in education. In *2019 IEEE Jordan International Joint Conference on Electrical Engineering and Information Technology (JEEIT)* (pp. 736-741). IEEE.

[16] Prakoso, A. F., Nurul, R., Wulandari, A., Trisnawati, N., Fitrayati, D., Rachmawati, L., & Andriansyah, E. H. (2017). Reliability, Responsiveness, Assurance, Empathy, and Tangible: Still Can Satisfy The Customer. International Journal of Business and Management Invention, 6(3), 68-75.

[17] Naim, A., Alahmari, F., & Rahim, A. (2021). Role of Artificial Intelligence in Market Development and Vehicular Communication. *Smart Antennas: Recent Trends in Design and Applications*, 2, 28.

[18] Hussain, M. R., Quadri, N. N., Ahmad, N., Qamar, S., Khan, N., Naim, A., & Hussain, M. E. (2019, April). Effective cost optimization approach in Healthcare to Minimize the treatment cost of Brain-tumor Patients. In *2019 International Conference on Computer and Information Sciences (ICCIS)* (pp. 1-5). IEEE.

[19] Naim, A., Sattar, R. A., Al Ahmary, N.., & Razwi, M. T. (2021) Implementation of Quality Matters Standards on Blended Courses: A Case Study. *FINANCE INDIA Indian Institute of Finance Vol. XXXV No. 3*, September 2021 Pages—873 – 890.

Chapter 5

Economies of Scale for Security Applications in Business

Arshi Naim[1,*] and Syed Zubairul Hassan[2,†]

[1]Department of Information Systems,
King Khalid University, Abha, Kingdom of Saudi Arabia (KSA)
[2]Shri Jai Narayan PG College, Lucknow, India

Abstract

This is an extended chapter, focusing on the economies of scale for the organizations dealing with the crucial issues of security systems in business operations. Economies of scale are achieved by managing the cost. Information Technology (IT) is an important and irreplaceable need of society and all working sector's success depends on IT to a greater extent; therefore maintaining security features is one of the most important aspects of IT. When security is discussed in any business sector, Patch Management (P.Mgnt) has to be taken under account and described in detail. P. Mgnt includes many concerns and areas to be described for IT security in business such as methods and problems in updating patch, methods of reducing security risks with P.Mgnt, methods of achieving economies of scale by controlling the operational costs and taking decisions in investing as and when necessary. This chapter presents a general definition of Patch management, its benefits and management of working cost through theoretical models, also the chapter

* Corresponding Author's Email: arshi@kku.edu.sa.
† Corresponding Author's Email: syedzubair996@gmail.com.

In: Competitive Trends and Technologies in Business Management
Editors: Arshi Naim and Praveen K. Malik
ISBN: 978-1-68507-612-2

gives methods of feeding techniques for microstrip patch antenna MPA, showing the contracting and non-contracting methods.

Keywords: operational cost, patch management, information technology, microstrip patch antenna, feeding techniques, economies of scale

Introduction

Business Operations have to preserve and maintain security because all the functions are applied by the help of IS /IT. Major security problems are due to errors in software; these issues are commonly known as vulnerabilities which can create or enhance the security concerns [1]. In the current scenario IT industry faces major security challenges causing serious sabotages especially for confidential data. In this situation investing in security applications for enhancing the security is not the choice but the need for most of the firms. Statistical data show that IT has a major objective to remove vulnerabilities because out of one thousand software codes, percentages of errors and mistakes are very high almost 20% of it. Below given figure is presenting the relevance of P. Mgnt as per IT in the system management [2, 4].

Benefits of P.Mgnt have many dimensions and it performs several jobs, some of them are maintaining current knowledge of available patches, deciding the patches that are suitable for particular systems, ensuring that patches are installed in a right way, testing systems after installation, and documenting all associated procedures [4, 21].

Like the health and security are important for all areas, the same implies for systems also, health refers to the well being of the systems and working without any errors and security means systems without vulnerabilities; the P.Mgnt is important in aiding to maintain the health and security of the systems that are being patched. Besides the patches are also used to bring software up to date to be compatible with the latest hardware, but this process requires good investment and therefore the costs are likely to increase to a good level. Organizations incur the cost in the optimal frequency of patch updates to make the balance of operational costs and damage costs related with security vulnerabilities [5].

Table 1. Examples of products for P.Mgnt [9]

Examples of Products Working to Automate Patch Management Tasks
Ring Master Software's APM
Manage Engine's Desktop Central
Central and SolarWinds Patch Manager.

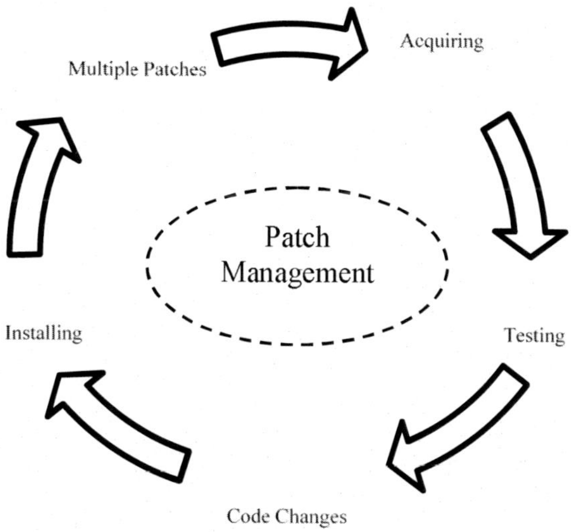

Figure 1. Relevance of P.Mgnt in Systems Management [1].

Literature Review

In the year 1950s, pioneer *Microstrip Antenna* (Ms.A) [23] was introduced but it took two decades to gain popularity and awareness for its use and benefits. Only after the development of printed circuit boards (PCB) in the 1970s, Ms.A got its recognition. Ms.A has many advantages such as light weight, low profile, low cost, planar configuration, easy of conformal, superior portability, suitable for array with the ease of fabrication and integration with microwave monolithic integrate circuits (MMICs) and after PCB these benefits were known and used at a greater extent. The applications of Ms.A are not limited to single areas but from official levels to personal levels, some of the examples are given in Figure 2 [7].

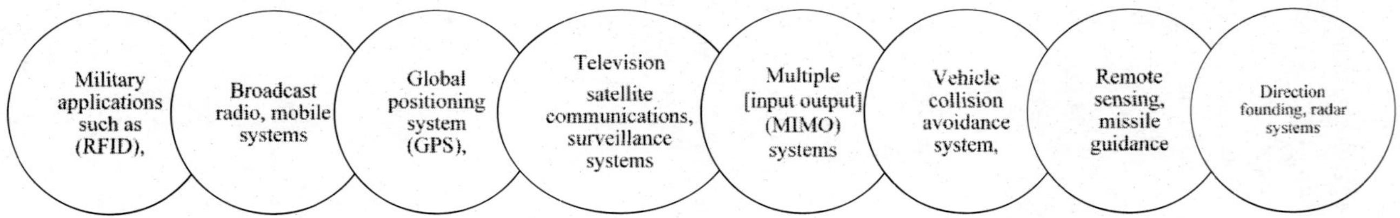

Figure 2. Applications of Ms.A [23].

Figure 2 shows the applications of Ms.A, but the applications are not restricted to these examples only, there are many more examples which are not covered in this chapter. Antenna is a transducer which transmits or receives electromagnetic waves. Ms.A has several advantages over conventional microwave antenna (Mw.A) and therefore it is used in a variety of practical applications. Ms.A has two sides in its design; one side has dielectric substrate and ground plane (GP) on another side.

To describe *Microstrip patch antenna* (MPA), it has non planar and planar geometry on one side of a dielectric substrate and a GP on other side [23]. MPA is used widely because of its planar configuration and ease of integration with microstrip technology. It is a printed resonant antenna for narrow-band microwave wireless links requiring semi-hemispherical coverage. The rectangular and circular patches are the basic and most commonly used MPA [23].

2.1. Feeding Techniques

There are many methods of feeding techniques for MPA, here we show the contracting and non-contracting methods and Figures 3 and 4 present the methods of feeding techniques for MPA.

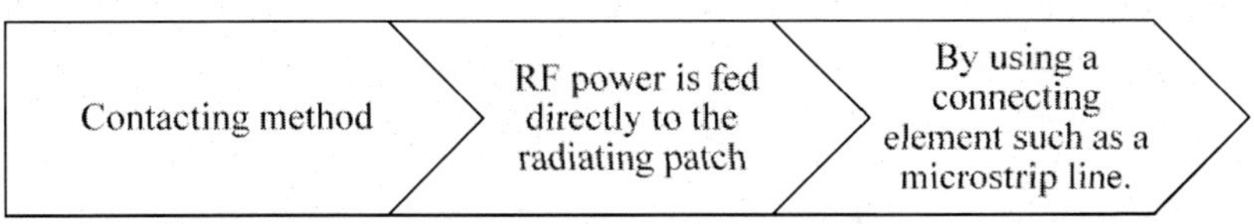

Figure 3. Contracting method.

In this method, the use of connecting elements like microstrip line is used for RF power which later is fed straight to the radiating patches.

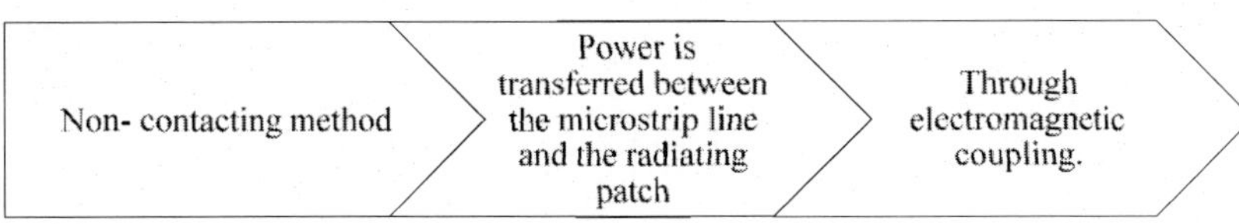

Figure 4. Non-contracting method [6, 7].

Electromagnetic coupling allows the transfer of power between the microstrip line and the radiating patch in a non-contracting method.

Table 2 shows the most popular feeding techniques; although as mentioned earlier there is many other techniques also which are not given in this Chapter.

Table 2. Four popular feeding techniques [17]

Popular Feeding Techniques
Microstrip line (Ms.L)
Coaxial probe (CP) (both contacting schemes)
Aperture Coupling (AC)
Proximity Coupling (PC) (both non-contacting schemes).

Discussion

(Ms. L) is a kind of feed arrangement that has the gain that the feed can be fixed on the same substrate to supply a planar structure and the conducting strip is smaller in width in contrast to patch. In Ms. L the conducting strip is connected in a straight line to the edge of the Ms. P.

(CP) is difficult to model and has the issue that it provides narrow bandwidth, in CP, the inner conductor of the coaxial connector widens throughout the dielectric and is soldered to the radiating patch (RP), while the outer conductor is coupled to the (GP). The major advantage of this is that the feed can be positioned at any of the required locations inside the patch in order to match with its input impedance.

In *(AC)* technique, the RP and the microstrip feed line are parted by the (GP). The patch and the feed line are coupled through a slot (CS) in the ground plane. This technique has multiple layers that cause an increase in thickness of the antenna. This aspect is considered to be the big flaw and disadvantage in the technique. Below given figure shows the process of this feeding technique.

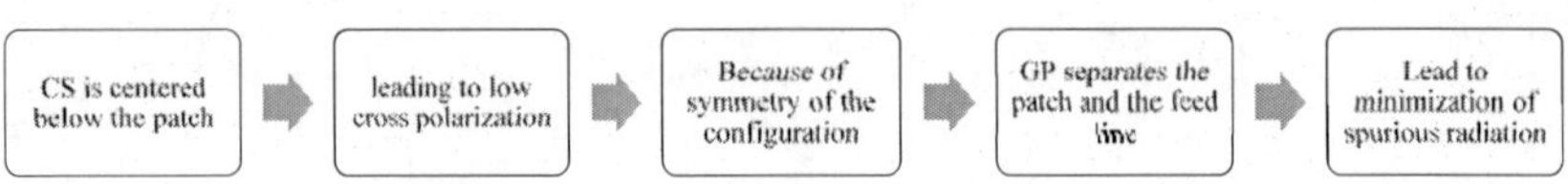

Figure 5. AC feeding technique [3, 6].

(PC) has another term which is electromagnetic coupling scheme that has two dielectric substrates which are applied between two substrates through a feed line. The (RP) is placed on top of the upper substrate which provides the benefits to this feed technique not only this it also offers high bandwidth. Table 3 shows the major benefit and disadvantage of this feeding technique.

Table 3. PC advantage and disadvantage

PC	
Advantages	**Disadvantage**
It is able to overcome and remove fake and suspicious feed radiation.	It has two dielectric layers which require good mapping; therefore it gives rise to complexity in fabrication.

Applications of Microsript Patch Antenna

Table 4. Description of applications of MPA [8]

Application	**Description**
GPSA	Microstrip patch antennas having high permittivity sintered substrate material for global positioning system (GPS). These antennas are circularly polarized and very compact.
RFID	RFID is used in different areas like mobile communication, logistics, manufacturing, transportation and health care. RFID system generally uses frequencies between 30 Hz and 5.8 GHz depending on its applications. Basically RFID system is a tag or transponder and a transceiver or reader.
WiMax	The IEEE 802.16 standard is known as WiMax. It can reach upto 30 mile radius theoretically and data rate 70 Mbps. Microstrip patch antenna generates three resonant modes at 2.7, 3.3 and 5.3 GHz and can, therefore, be used in WiMax compliant communication equipment.
RA	Radar can be used for detecting moving targets such as people and vehicles. The microstrip antennas are an ideal choice. The fabrication technology based on photolithography enables the bulk production of microstrip antenna with repeatable performance at a lower cost in a lesser time frame as compared to the conventional antennas.
MPBA	The microstrip antenna operates in the 2400 to 2484 MHz ISM Band.
MSPWC	This is a single-patch broadband microstrip S-shaped patch antenna. Microstrip S-shaped patch antenna is fed by a coaxial feeding. The antenna is designed by inserting two slots into rotated square patch then it look like English letter 'S'. Because of the slots and thick substrate, bandwidth of antenna is increased.

The microstrip patch antennas (MPA) are well known for their performance and strong design [12, 23]. MPA has applications in various fields such as in the medical field, satellites, military systems, rockets, aircrafts missiles and many more. In the current situation these applications are growing for several commercial features also especially for the cost optimization options for different substrate materials and production. MPA has a number of applications and some of these applications are given in Figure 6 and described in Table 4.

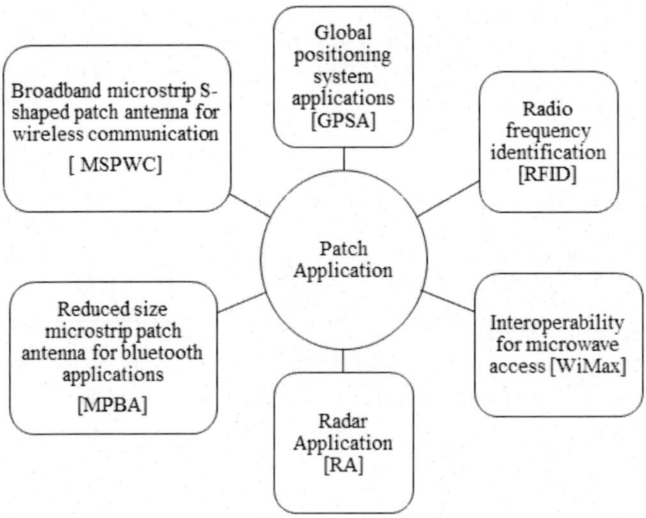

Figure 6. Applications of MPA [8].

Working of P.Mgnt

The working and application of P.Mgnt depends on the condition if patch is used to a standalone system or on a system for corporate networks. Figure 7 given below explains both the cases; standalone system and corporate network [10].

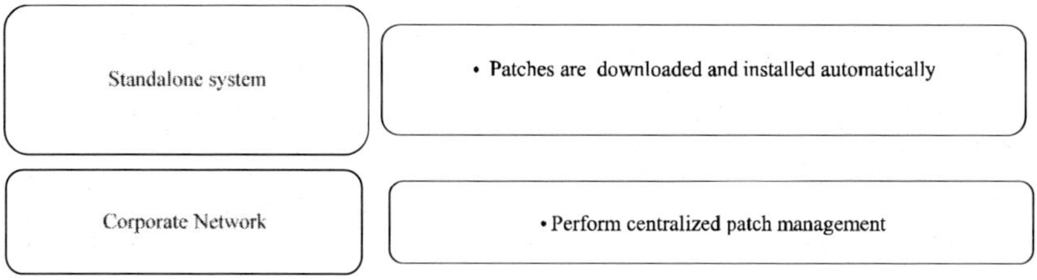

Figure 7. Application of Patch Mgnt for two cases [16, 17].

The case of Stand-alone system is automatic condition where the operating system and the applications on that system perform an automatic check on regular basis and find the availability of patches, in case of new patches are found, the system downloads them automatically. In case of corporate situation; P.Mgnt works in a different way because firms have to keep the stability and consistency for all machines therefore automatic download is not feasible even if updated patches are available. In most of the situation organizations execute the centralized approach than of allowing machines to download the patches by themselves. Below given figure shows the P.Mgnt for corporate network [13].

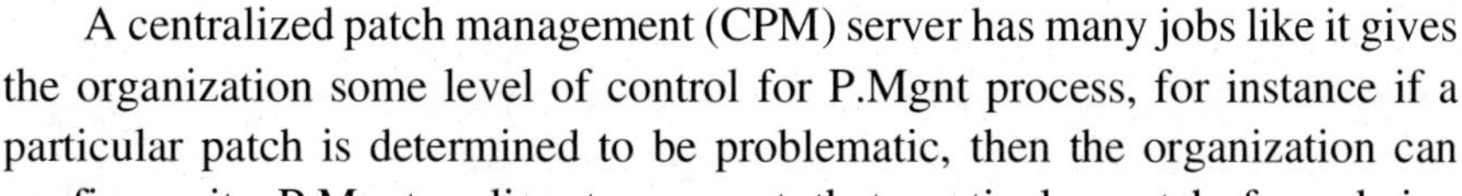

Figure 8. Working of P. Mgnt for corporate network [13].

A centralized patch management (CPM) server has many jobs like it gives the organization some level of control for P.Mgnt process, for instance if a particular patch is determined to be problematic, then the organization can configure its P.Mgnt policy to prevent that particular patch from being deployed instead of automating the P. Mgnt.

CPM provides many advantages for the firm like retaining the internet bandwidth, which is described as the advantage for the organization because it omits the need for all systems to download the similar patch rather it helps in downloading once and distributing for all the other systems in the firm. This is an ideal condition but does not mean that all organizations would follow the same strategy for P.Mgnt, some firms prefer to hire professionals for the security management and others refer to apply different network management services.

Most of the software companies in fixed intervals provide patches for their security benefits. There are basically three main purposes for the firms to release new patches for their products, figure given below presents these three purposes and Table 5 gives the brief description of each purpose.

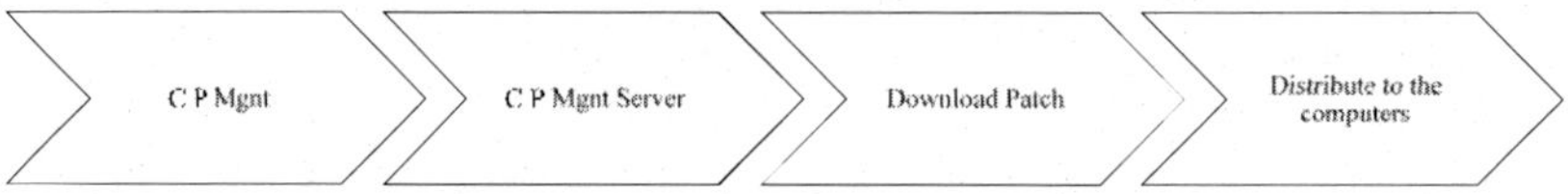

Figure 9. Three primary purposes of P.Mgnt [5, 13.

Table 5. Description of purposes of P.Mgnt [14, 15]

Description
Hackers are always in the look out of weak securities or vulnerable situations and the applications of Patches are to address security vulnerabilities, therefore if any such situation is identified or present in form of security risk then it is the responsibility of the vendors to work and control risk by issuing the patch to remove risks in the products.
Sometimes during the validation stage certain bugs are discovered so if the firm does not release patch to fix the problem it may lead to more serious issues of security. These preventive measures give two benefits; first to increase software working with reliability and another is to stop future security risk.
Quality management is always an important aim of all the software firms and for improving the existing feature or introducing the new firms would require to offer patches for better working, better security and even for updating the systems.

Patches may not have benefits all the time, there are many common problems such as [4, 17] Buggy Patch; new problems cannot be known before being be initiated by patches. New Problems are introduced by the implementation of patch which otherwise were not present in the previous systems, Patches are deployed without being tested for bugs or any other compatible issues for the software system, Patches are not received timely and Patches are not updated or released for the new products.

Patch Management Life Cycle

It is the work of firms to take testing under consideration before the release as well as deploying it at all the levels of organization. The IT department has to play the major role in P.Mgnt for conducting the test within the sandbox (SB) environment, this may result in controlling the problem of security and the production system will not get affected due to any loophole in P.Mgnt [13]. The IT department has to take many optional methods to maintain the security with any issues, the following figure shows those options.

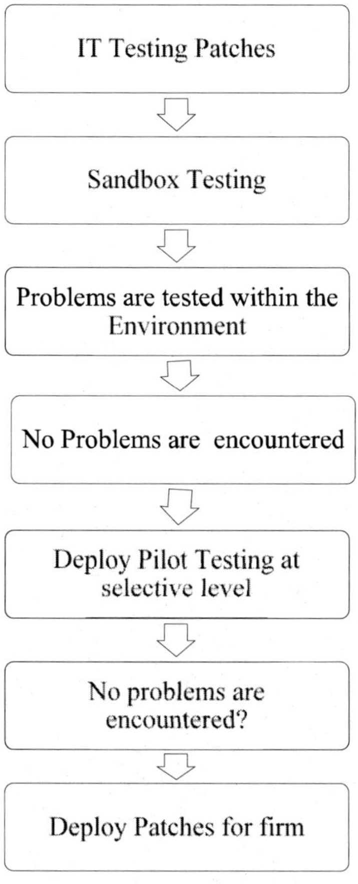

Figure 10. IT P.Mgnt for the Firms [13].

Results may vary from the testing to the real deployment of patches, however it is not a common scenario but sometimes patches are identified for causing the issues to the production systems; in this situation firms have to take a decision to remove the patch to maintain the security systems. P.Mgnt is not an easy function; IT department has to take complex decisions on releasing, updating and deploying the patches also issues are witnessed on receiving the patches for the firm as and when needed. There are simple to complicated decisions IT has to take for the application of Patches for the Production systems. The IT recommends some suggestions for the P.Mgnt following table describes the recommendations for P.Mgnt for the firm.

Table 6. P.Mgnt recommendations [12, 13]

Recommendation for P.Mgnt
Develop one Patch and Vulnerability Group (PVG) in small firms
Large firms to monitor and responsible for the execution of Patches
Large firm assign some team members for creating and deploying of these Patches and study PVG
Separate IT team with complete autonomy should work for the P.Mgnt and study the vulnerabilities.
Only IT team members should be responsible for the implementation.

The PVG is charged with a number of responsibilities, not least of which is taking inventory of all the IT resources in the company's system. It's important to capture hardware, which may require firmware updates, and software, including applications and operating systems. This puts them in a good position and be responsible for monitoring for updates and patches for this equipment.

Prioritizing the order of implementation of the patches is also PVG responsibility. Hopefully, if the company has the resources for the PVG to create a database as a repository for this information so all the patches/ remediation can be logged somewhere accessible to those who need to know about them. Most of the firms apply the following process for the P. Mgnt which is given in figure below:

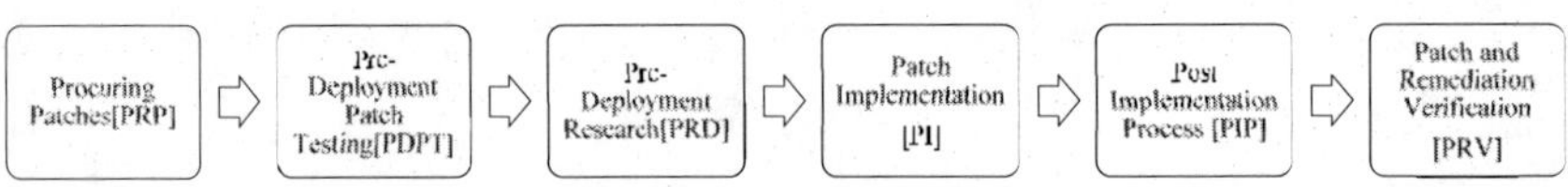

Figure 11. Process of Procure and use of Patches [10].

PRP

Purchase/obtain the real patches from any of the sources like downloading from the websites or other distributors. Although there are methods of automation for obtaining patches, it is relevant to check the authenticity of the patches; to do that PVG has to carefully be analyzed and then patches should be determined.

This process is not an easy process; PVG tests the virus and bug and makes sure for error free and no infection in patches. Firms can use a few easy methods to do so like updating the software, installing the licensed antivirus and updating it regularly. Hackers' mischief and attempt to make unauthorized access cannot be avoided but such applications can provide multi-layering in the security systems for patches.

PDPT

Before deploying the Patches, certain measures are recommended for the firms to apply because just implementing the new patch and replacing the old one does not necessarily enhance the security systems and it is not an easy process too therefore before using the patch for the real system, it is used for non-production for testing. If testing doesn't encounter any problem, the deployment can be carried out smoothly. This pre testing is very important to avoid risks of crashing of systems or other major problems. This Chapter has mentioned two types of test environment for pre using of patches; such as SD testing for the environment and Pilot testing for the same specifications for the systems.

PDR

Sometimes firms have to meet the deadlines and do not have time or even infrastructure to conduct pre testing, in such situations previous studies and researches are very helpful for knowing the reasons and solutions for P.Mgnt. This existing research provides benefits and disadvantages of deploying the patches for the production systems, methods, and other necessary recommendations.

PDR elaborates the criteria and conditions to examine for describing and obtaining the patches, also provides reviews of threats, risks and other major issues apart from the results caused by the implementation of patches. Operational cost is also studied in PDR and gives details on how to maintain economies of scale for the future.

PI

If PI works in phases, chances of crash and other risks associated with patches are reduced, also it is not mandatory to consider the size of the firm, therefore if PVG is conducted and patches are first manually implemented followed by the automation, it may result in better functioning of the system. Firms should apply patches for the entire system to defend all security threats and risks.

PIP

The IT department of a firm can use the approach of PVG for communication of information for solutions, and types of vulnerabilities for the existing systems. This method will lead to the IT team members to handle the critical issues without major administrative hurdles because the entire firm will be well distributed with the information about PVG. Besides dealing with the technical issues PVG also deals with administrative decisions on allocating cost for patches in the financial budget.

PRV

Implementation is not the last stage but to check whether the applied patches are working successfully for enhancing the security or not and also if its cost effect or not, therefore PVG offers all possible options for the good working of patches. PRV accounts on first results of testing on non-production system before commercializing at the real production system for the firm, apart from these there are few more methods for the verification of patches like verifying the documents of service providers, checking for the specifications, compatibility followed by checking the process of installation, correctness and effective testing on the systems.

Cost Management for P.Mgnt

Cost management for P.Mgnt focuses on methods of cost optimization, mostly cost increases for P.Mgnt due to two reasons, firstly when firm shows reluctance in investing in updating when the patches are released and important to be deployed and secondly when service providers wait for the identification of vulnerabilities [5, 11]. Both situations cause an increase in cost investment and firms have to take immediate application to maintain the security for the systems.

Achieving the economies of scale is important management issues for types of firms and when we explain this for the IT sector, two types of cost in patch management are required [11].

a) Cost incurred as a remedy of damage
b) Cost incurred for the update

Firms have to invest more monetary inputs for the situation when security is not examined and existence of vulnerabilities are not patched causing major damage in the system. Another manor investment that a firm has to make on a regular basis is on updating, testing and installing the patches.

Cost management for the P.Mgnt is also a complex decision making process for the firms because occasionally remedial investment in updating or deploying new patches can cause other problems in product management.

The last part of the Chapter deals with the cost management for P.Mgnt that includes various decisions for the firm. These decisions are given in Figure 12.

Here the firms need to take the decisions on cost affectivity and tradeoff for security, therefore cost ratio analysis is done to evaluate if investment should be done for release of new packets, update the packets or install the packets or to compromise on security for product management. Here the decision is also based on the value and relevance of security in comparison to the investment necessary for the patches; also it depends on the affordability of the firms to invest more cost especially for small scale organizations.

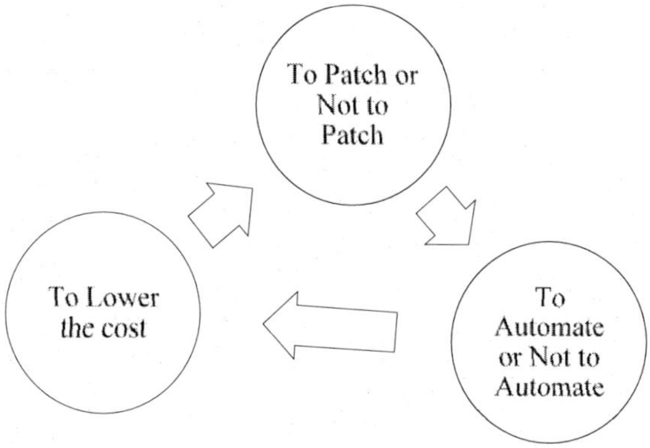

Figure 12. Cost management decisions for P.Mgnt [11].

Firms make comparative analyses between automation and manual control to decide cost investment decisions [11]. The decision is based on the annual report for cost and benefit ratio between the two options to automate or manually deploy the patches [18, 19].

Most of the time avoiding cost increment cannot be controlled and as mentioned earlier small firms are unable to increase the investment in the budget for IT sector, in this situation firms have to compromise on other grounds, which are usually based on low cost solutions [11, 19]. These low cost solutions include, introduction of security at managerial levels, reducing cost for other infrastructure such as cost for material. However these solutions are not appropriate because software vulnerabilities can effectively be solved through deployment of patches, in this situation, the most suitable solution for the firm is to share the cost of software products. This method seems to be directed for cost optimization but the software experts question this type of solution for its implication. If the bugs or vulnerabilities are due to any faulty issues in the program and software firms are accountable for that, then further investment in P.Mgnt is not justified and cost should be borne by the software firms. Software experts suggest sharing of liabilities in this scenario and the types of methods to overcome cyber security challenges [17].

Results

The results show that business management use many applications and have crucial issues of software securities but their vulnerabilities are best solved by the deployment of patches. In this case the firms have to make some complex decisions on when and how patches should be applied. There are many methods of feeding techniques for MPA, but this chapter has shown two important methods; contracting and non-contracting methods for the firms for their business operations. Ms.A has its application in varied sectors and the working and application of P.Mgnt depends on the condition if patch is used on a standalone system or on a system for corporate networks. Conditions and working of Patches are defined for both the conditions. This chapter also shows the working of Patch management life cycle and why firms have to take testing under consideration before the release as well as the deployment of patches at all levels of organization. The study offers recommendation for P.Mgnt for the IT firms for adopting the process of procure and use of Patches. Finally cost management for P.Mgnt is described with the reasons for why cost investment is made for P.Mgnt and what the major decisions are firms have to take for cost optimization. Last but not the least the chapter gives a brief recommendation by the software experts in the field of cost management for P.Mgnt for effective working and how to increase profit for the business firms.

Conclusion

This chapter is a qualitative chapter showing the general scenario of P.Mgnt that can facilitate the firms in overall management, understanding the benefits and disadvantages of P. Mgnt, and why Patches are important, the process of P.Mgnt and its cost management.

References

[1] Dey, D., Lahiri, A., & Zhang, G. (2015). Optimal policies for security patch management. *INFORMS Journal on Computing,* 27(3), 462-477.

[2] Martini, B., & Choo, K. K. R. (2014). Building the next generation of cyber security professionals. Martini B and Choo KK R.

[3] Wang, B., Li, X., de Aguiar, L. P., Menasche, D. S., & Shafiq, Z. (2017). Characterizing and modeling patching practices of industrial control systems. *Proceedings of the ACM on Measurement and Analysis of Computing Systems,* 1(1), 1-23.

[4] Naim, A., & Alahmari, F. (2020). Reference model of e-learning and quality to establish interoperability in higher education systems. *International Journal of Emerging Technologies in Learning (iJET), 15*(2), 15-28.

[5] Force, J. T. (2017). Security and Privacy Controls for Information Systems and Organizations (No. NIST Special Publication (SP) 800-53 Rev. 5 (Draft)). National Institute of Standards and Technology.

[6] Naim, A., Hussain, M. R., Naveed, Q. N., Ahmad, N., Qamar, S., Khan, N., & Hweij, T. A. (2019, April). Ensuring interoperability of e-learning and quality development in education. In *2019 IEEE Jordan International Joint Conference on Electrical Engineering and Information Technology (JEEIT)* (pp. 736-741). IEEE.

[7] Chatterjee, S., & Thekdi, S. (2020). An iterative learning and inference approach to managing dynamic cyber vulnerabilities of complex systems. *Reliability engineering & system safety,* 193, 106664.

[8] Alshawish, A., & de Meer, H. (2019, June). Risk-based decision-support for vulnerability remediation in electric power networks. In *Proceedings of the Tenth ACM International Conference on Future Energy Systems* (pp. 378-380).

[9] Souppaya, M., & Scarfone, K. (2013). Guide to enterprise patch management technologies. *NIST Special Publication,* 800, 40.

[10] Hassani, P. (2020). Implementing Patch Management Process.

[11] Naim, A., Alahmari, F., & Rahim, A. (2021). Role of Artificial Intelligence in Market Development and Vehicular Communication. *Smart Antennas: Recent Trends in Design and Applications*, 2, 28.

[12] Gauci, A., Michelin, S., & Salles, M. (2017). Addressing the challenge of cyber security maintenance through patch management. *CIRED-Open Access Proceedings Journal,* 2017(1), 2599-2601.

[13] Sihvonen, H. M., & Jäntti, M. (2010, August). Improving release and patch management processes: An empirical case study on process challenges. In *2010 Fifth International Conference on Software Engineering Advances* (pp. 232-237). *IEEE.*

[14] Segre, H., Carmel, Y., Segoli, M., Tchetchik, A., Renan, I., Perevolotsky, A., & Shwartz, A. (2019). Cost-effectiveness of uncultivated field-margins and semi-natural patches in Mediterranean areas: A multi-taxa, landscape scale approach. *Biological Conservation,* 240, 108262.

[15] Naim, A., Sattar, R. A., Al Ahmary, N.., & Razwi, M. T. (2021) Implementation of Quality Matters Standards on Blended Courses: A Case Study. FINANCE INDIA Indian Institute of Finance Vol. XXXV No. 3, September 2021 Pages—873 – 890.

[16] Nunez, Y., Gustavson, F., Grossman, F., & Tappert, C. (2010, June). Designing a distributed patch management security system. In *2010 International Conference on Information Society* (pp. 162-167). IEEE.

[17] Hussain, M. R., Quadri, N. N., Ahmad, N., Qamar, S., Khan, N., Naim, A., & Hussain, M. E. (2019, April). Effective cost optimization approach in Healthcare to minimize the treatment cost of Brain-tumor Patients. In *2019 International Conference on Computer and Information Sciences (ICCIS)* (pp. 1-5). IEEE.

[18] Song, K. T., Kim, S. I., & Kim, S. H. (2021). A Design of Improvement Method of Central Patch Controlled Security Platform Using Blockchain. In *Advances in Computer Science and Ubiquitous Computing* (pp. 555-561). Springer, Singapore.

[19] Dissanayake, N., Jayatilaka, A., Zahedi, M., & Babar, M. A. (2020). Software Security Patch Management - A Systematic Literature Review of Challenges, Approaches, Tools and Practices. arXiv preprint arXiv:2012.00544.

[20] Mohlenhoff, K. A., & Codding, B. F. (2017). When does it pay to invest in a patch? The evolution of intentional niche construction. *Evolutionary Anthropology: Issues, News, and Reviews,* 26(5), 218-227.

[21] Lee, J. H., & Kim, H. (2017). Security and privacy challenges in the internet of things [security and privacy matters]. *IEEE Consumer Electronics Magazine,* 6(3), 134-136.

[22] Gauci, A., Michelin, S., & Salles, M. (2017). Addressing the challenge of cyber security maintenance through patch management. *CIRED-Open Access Proceedings Journal,* 2017(1), 2599-2601.

[23] Kim, J., Sohn, M., & Won, Y. (2017). An Automatic Patch Management System with Improved Security. In *Advanced Multimedia and Ubiquitous Engineering* (pp. 74-80). Springer, Singapore.

[24] Monperrus, M. (2014, May). A critical review of" automatic patch generation learned from human-written patches": Essay on the problem statement and the evaluation of automatic software repair. In *Proceedings of the 36th International Conference on Software Engineering* (pp. 234-242).

[25] DeLuzio, C. (2019). *Procurement Guide for Better Election Cybersecurity.* New York: New York University School of Law.

[26] Naim, A. (2021). Application of Quality Matters in Digital Learning in Higher Education. *Texas Journal of Multidisciplinary Studies*, *1*(1), 3-12.

[27] Humble, J., & Farley, D. (2010). *Continuous delivery: reliable software releases through build, test, and deployment automation.* Pearson Education.

[28] Sotres, P., Santana, J. R., Sánchez, L., Lanza, J., & Muñoz, L. (2017). Practical lessons from the deployment and management of a smart city internet-of-things infrastructure: The smartsantander testbed case. *IEEE Access,* 5, 14309-14322.

[29] Kaur, N., & Malhotra, S. (2016, October). A review on significance of design parameters of microstrip patch antennas. In *2016 5th International Conference on Wireless Networks and Embedded Systems (WECON)* (pp. 1-6). IEEE.

[30] Naim, A., Khan, M. F., Hussain, M. R., & Khan, N. (2019). "Virtual Doctor" Management Technique in the Diagnosis of ENT Diseases. *JOE,* 15(9), 88.

Chapter 6

Virtual Learning in Business Information Systems: A Case Study on Quality Matters Applications

Arshi Naim*

Department of Information Systems, King Khalid University,
Abha, Kingdom of Saudi Arabia (KSA)

Abstract

E-Learning has contributed to the great extent in imparting the education in the crucial time for COVID-19. This is the extended research work presenting the applications of broad multidimensional reference model of Quality Matters for E-Learning standards for blended courses and full online courses in such a way that learning outcomes of the module could be met. In this research paper the importance and tasks of Quality Matters for the course development and its relationship with E-Learning was defined and analyzed in the learning environment with special reference to Public University (PU) in Gulf for undergraduate students in Business Management curriculum. This study clearly defined that the Reference Model of Quality Matters for E- Learning standards could be applied for all types of Modules such as Supportive, Blended or Full Online in learning paradigm that aid in meeting learning outcomes of the business courses. Also this study magnified the patterns how QM standards facilitated E-Learning. The reference model of Quality Matters can be applied for all types of modules and program.

* Corresponding Author's Email: arshi@kku.edu.sa.

In: Competitive Trends and Technologies in Business Management
Editors: Arshi Naim and Praveen K. Malik
ISBN: 978-1-68507-612-2

Keywords: quality matters, e-learning standards, blended module, learning management services, e-learning deanship

1. Introduction

In online settings, teachers and students bring assumptions about how classes' work that are based on face-to-face models of teaching and learning that can be moved to online environment. Public University (PU) in Middle East introduced an e-learning centre in 2005 and in 2008 pioneered Blackboard CollaborateTM [BBCL] to achieve local and international online education. E-Learning [EL] with Quality Matters in PU put efforts to organize, build and construct learning modules at an international level. For example in this view in 2011 and 2012 E-Learning introduced Public University E-Learning (PUEL) for achieving international standards for learning Modules while applying Quality Matters (QM rubrics) [1] with an objective to new learning and teaching practices. New technologies and resources for interaction, teaching and learning are appearing every day and transforming the potential for new teaching practices. A teacher engaged with thinking about, experimenting with and continuously developing their technical and social practices. Online teaching can be a boon for teachers themselves, making it possible for educators, like their students, to have access to the professional resources they need to continue to learn. If online professional development is taken seriously and done right, every teacher, novice and experienced, could have the opportunity to learn from the best. Online courses also provide a powerful way to enhance teachers' opportunities for quality professional development. Quality Matters is a continuous improvement model for assuring the quality of online courses through a faculty review process which furnishes rubrics for Online and Hybrid courses [2]. PU attempts to appraise the learning modules at par with international standards while fulfilling the essential standards of Quality Matters. This study has shown how the blended learning modules and full online applied QM standards and successfully achieved for the graduate's outcomes.

2. Literature Review

A feature that is particularly relevant to PU's gender separated population is the ability to provide instantaneous collaboration through the operation of instant messaging on BBCl enterprise [3]. This has enabled students and teachers to work together in an informal "virtual environment," therefore they are able to chat, connect through video to have one-to-one interviews, and share their desktops with one another to exchange ideas; an enhancement to communication in all the perspective [4]. Over 7,000 students across 25 departments, including medicine, pharmacy, dentistry, computer sciences, engineering, education, Sharia and religion, training, and more are adopting online collaboration into their prospectus today[5]. In 2005, the university established its first EL centre and in 2008, chose BBCl to integrate with the university's primary LMS, Blackboard Learn™. Mohammad Qatrawi, Research and Development Manager at the EL Center at PU state "Choosing online collaboration was a strategic decision [5]." It provides equal chances for all, quality, and better student experiences and keeps us up to date with best practices [6]. So, BBCl was used to support achieving EL vision [7]". With this idea on education, many of the facet and capabilities of the BBCl™ online collaboration platform are assisting PU with its EL vision. Most widely used capabilities are web conferencing for hosting virtual classrooms, the whiteboard for making classes more engaging and interactive, polling for answering questions, and instant messaging [7]. The increase in adoption has been driven by their 'top–down' vision where instructors are comprehensively trained either face-to-face or more often, online. All of the content and training materials are published on the university's EL Deanship website and EL specialists can be reached practically to help students requiring backing [7]. PUEL has adopted Learning Management Services for providing online platform for imparting knowledge and assessments. Figure 1 shows historical and trends of application of LMS for various benefits such as software demonstration, education sector, sharing learning resources, developing courses, making announcements, communicating with the participants, etc. Figure 1 has covered some of the features of LMS from the past.

In general E-learning (EL) is not a new concept it was started way back in 1924. During this time EL focused mostly on the basic communication skills and for conducting assessments through the medium of distant learning education. With the development of computer based training in 1980, EL witnessed a drastic development in education section. Below given Figure 2 provides concise but comprehensive stages of development of EL.

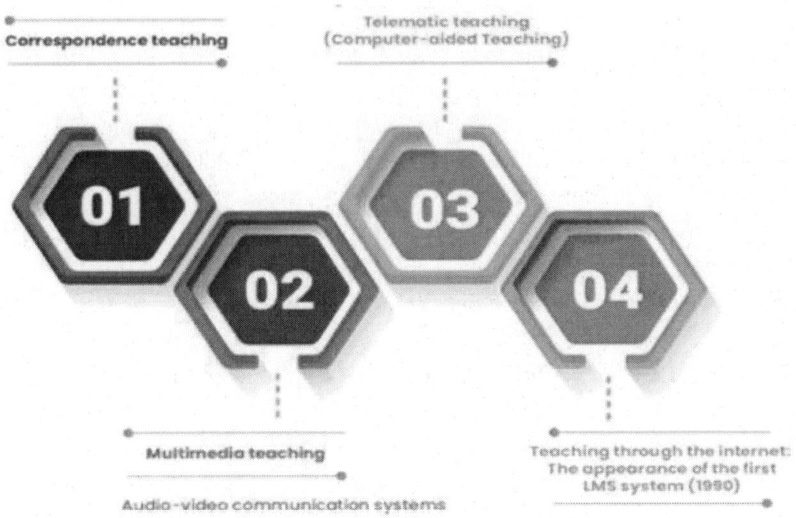

Figure 1. History and trends of LMS [7].

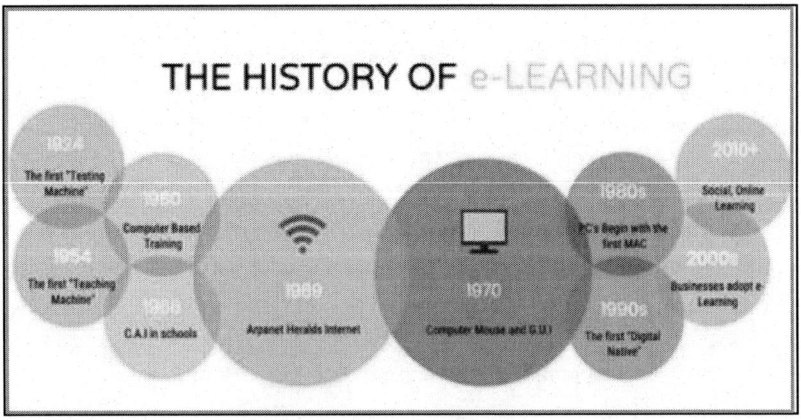

Figure 2. History of EL [8].

E-learning is being originated as a fundamental scope of the student learning experience in H.E. It is no longer core business only for those universities with a mission for distance education, its financially and economically affordable and can be organized in a systematic as well as in integrated methods therefore many universities in US, UK and Australian Learning and Teaching Council in Australia focus more on relevance of virtual learning [8].

Many researches are conducted in the past to analyze the students' learning experience through EL and more than two decades compared the aspects associated with F2F learning over digital learning [9]. The comparative studies show relevance in terms of financial and economic feasibilities without hurdles in the meeting of course learning outcomes also there are evidences showing EL effectiveness with the application of reference models such as QM that we covered in this research paper, where we clearly showed how students' centric approach can be implemented on EL through the applications of rubrics of QM. Many researchers have defined EL as information and communication technologies used to support students improve their learning such as (Higher Education Funding Council of England, 2005) and the results show that good course design will enhance online learning [9].

Past studies also explain the financial and economic stabilities of universities or H.E. with the El platform for imparting teaching. In this regard researchers focus on four criteria, namely, interactivity, approaches to e-moderating, issues related to course design, and workload awareness [10].

Quality Matters (QM) started with a small group of colleagues in the MarylandOnline, Inc. (MOL) consortium [10]. These people researched to identify the issues for quality learning in academies, finding solutions for these issues and developed a structural framework to ensure quality of module. In the year 2003 MOL listed the methods of QM program that was able to develop the measurable procedure of quality assurance (QA) and request for funds from the academies for QA. This financial assistance was applied for the Improvement of Postsecondary Education (FIPSE) [11] grant from the U.S. Department of Education. QM set the following framework for developing courses with QA standards.

QM is a presitigious international society that ensures the best E-learning practices and gurantess the completion and achievement of learning outomes. Table given below explains all the framework of QM briefly. These framwork if applies by any academy for the QM practices of any module development, it is assumed that the module has execellent learning materials, assessment methods are alligned with the activities in an online environment or in traditional environment.

Online classes, hybrid or blended classes, and web-facilitated classes all employ online materials, which instructors and students are using at ever-increasing rates. Accordingly, instructors should continuously evaluate the effectiveness of such online materials. This paper sets forth the author's initial attempts to analyze a business course pursuant to items in the Quality Matters

(QM)™ Rubric designed by an organization whose mission is to certify the quality of online and blended courses.[12]

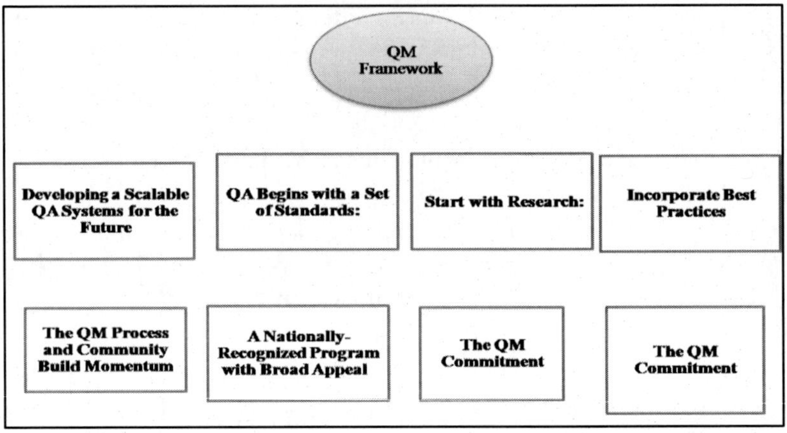

Figure 3. Framework of QM [11].

3. Methodology/Discussion

This research was descriptive in nature yet few standards for the course were scaled on likert. On the likert Scale 5 degree had been allotted to the levels from highly functional to poorly functional. PU E-Learning deanship assigns a peer reviewer for measuring the standards of Quality matters on blended courses and full online courses.

This paper discusses the application of QM rubrics in course development and the process of applications for full online courses as well as for blended courses.

Application of QM standards in online courses benefit the academy in several ways, this justification can be explained in terms of economies of scale not necessarily related with the direct financial gain. PU used the stimulus of EL to achieve the benefit of improving teaching pedagogy on digital platform by encouraging using QM standards, as a result this investment in QM consequence in various benefits such as quality driven modules, accredited course development, resource sharing options, training and guideline for other instructors to develop the modules on the same systems, achieving international acclaimed learning and teaching practices, etc. This investment by the academy has brought intangible profits and image building in the long term.

The substance of economies of scale derives from learning by doing, and this adds a dynamic element to an otherwise essentially static concept. PU has to input some measures in QM application in EL but in return, online instructors get trained and expert in online course development and online teaching practices while applying several models or rubrics. Below given procedure show how QM rubrics were applied successfully on blended modules.

It is practical to conclude how economies of scales worked in public academies without referring to the financial terms. As mentioned above PU achieved excellence and other intangible advantages through QM application in EL and below given case study discuss more on this findings showing how QM rubrics were applied on different tools and features of EL and successfully developed online module for students at large by having global presence and exploiting the optimum of IT.

PU's e-learning (PUEL) consisted four sections, entry point for the course named as Start Here, Project Page that described most important page in instructor had to describe and instructions about the course, Tasks elaborated list of detailed helping material that were required to achieve the QM standards for the Online as well as for Supportive Modules lastly Learner Support where instructor was to elaborate all issues pertaining to technical or problems related to learning. Blended Learning Modules are developed under 7 tasks sections, Introduction, Course Proposal, Start here, Syllabus, Are You an Online teacher, Sample unit, Learner Centric, Assessment and Final Thought and its learning outcomes were measured by using likert scale by the E-Learning peer reviews. For the purpose of study one of the Business Information Systems (BIS) modules was chosen. The name of the module was E-Commerce which was taught as a blended as well as full online course.

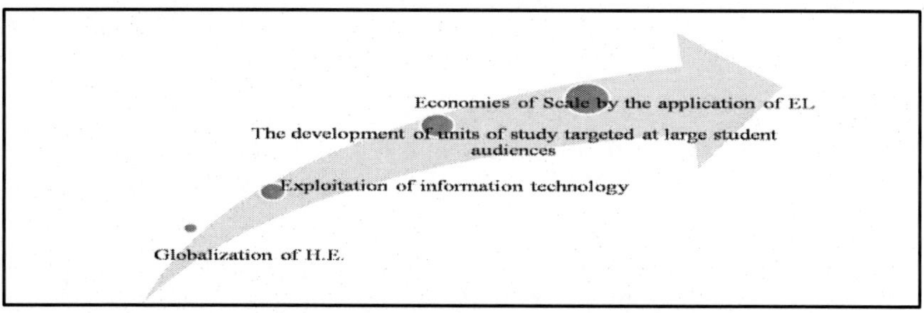

Figure 4. Economies of scale and scope in e-learning in PU [13].

Proposal for the blended module had to be submitted as Course Plan QM with PUEL peer review to evaluate the Learning Module on the guidelines given in Course Plan.

Start here was the task where QM requested to make an entry point elaborating all vital details of blended learning modules such as Welcome Message, Introduction, Course Description, Goals and Learning Outcomes, Course Structure, Course Outline, Readings References, Assessment and Grading and Assignments.

Syllabus was a highly structured guideline which elaborated the course content and methodology of program of study, reading reference, breakdown of assessment and other minute details. Considering these aspects we presented the course syllabus for Ecommerce with perspective of the students therefore we had put concise, simple, logical yet comprehensive content relevant for the student's knowledge. For the preparation of Syllabus as QM standards following features had been accounted that made the syllabus as most appropriate for meeting learning outcomes of the modules. Course Description, Course Co- requisite, Course pre – requisite, Goals and Learning Outcomes of the Modules, Course outline, Topic wise learning objectives, Basic information about course instructors, communication medium between instructor and students, teaching pedagogy, reading references, any rubrics for learning the course, Assessment Methods, Grading Policy, and netiquettes.

In the note "Are you an online teacher", as per PUEL and QM an instructor had to file proof and information explaining how effective her online teaching pedagogy was and how she was so successful in delivering quality learning material. Ecommerce was offered as a blended course as well as a full online course, where 30% was through online learning and 70% was through face to face learning before COVID-19 situation then this course was instructed in a full online medium. We got experience as online instructors for this course and we satisfactorily organized the principles of giving on line education. For uploading Course Contents and annotations, we used Lectures tool content type as PPT or PDF document. Announcement tool was used for urgent and instant notifications. We used course mail for selective notification. Uploaded E- Quiz and E- Exam Assignment tools then provided detailed steps to access the e-exam with all its prerequisites. For short and analytical case studies, used Discussion board where our students very devotedly participated through creating threads on that. To manage our course effectively, we created online Start here tool, from where students were easily able to take a journey to know all the minute details of the course, Grading policy, Pre- requisite and Co – requisite for the course, etc. We enjoyed giving online session on

Blackboard collaborate and on Elluminate live; students experienced new method to learn, to communicate and response to the queries. On Blackboard collaborate and Elluminate live we used an option to record our lectures too and students could get back to the lecture and listen many times to comprehend better. It was found that E- learning was a good way for an effective time management principle.

Sample Unit described the methodology of explaining and other course material delivery by the course instructor.

Ecommerce was a blended course where 30% of the course was to be given online and 70% given to face to face before pandemic and in current situation it was given as 100% online. Entire course of Ecommerce comprised nine chapters scheduled to be completed in 12 weeks. Table 1 presents the sample how week wise teaching pedagogy for online course is designed during pandemic.

Content Type [13] was to describe the contents of chapter 8: PPT, link of PDF, Video, and, Lecture's Handouts, Images on Blackboard before the online Session whole contents were uploaded on lecture Tool and announced on Announcement Tool. Face to face session on regular schedule was given on chapter 8 as well as Online live and recording lecture was conducted for chapter 8 therefore Timings, Navigating clue and other details were clearly declared on announcement prior to online session. After concluding chapter eight learning outcomes were achieved followed by completion of Activities (Assignment) for meeting objectives of Assessment.

Table 1. Teaching Pedagogy Learning Module Ecommerce

Week # 05 Online Learning	**Learning Outcomes**	**Online Activities**	**Online Assessment**
Work Impact on Employment Fears and Questions The Impact on Employment The Work Environment Employee Crime Employee Monitoring	Recognize the Fears and Questions Analyze the Impact on Employment Evaluate the Work Environment Explain Employee Crime Illustrate Employee Monitoring	Discussion: - Does the value of informing the public of controversial and sensitive information outweigh the dangers and risks? Discuss 5 reasons to support your answer	Discussion Forum Exam Quiz

Table 2. Assessment methods for blended learning module ecommerce

Online Assessment Methods	Learning Learning Outcomes
Online Discussion Forum	Enhance Communication and analytical skills
Online Case Study	Enhance logical thinking, comprehend contingencies and illustrate examples to support solution
Online Group Presentation	Enhance Communication skills, develop team spirit, build up coordination and impose learning by presenting
Online Quizzes	Enhance knowledge and cognitive skills
Online Exams	Enhance Enhance knowledge and cognitive skills

Activities [14] were uploaded on the Discussion Board and on Assignment tool with clear instructions on Announcement Tool. Finally all activities were assessed and a weighted total was uploaded on Full Grade Center.

Learners Centric Approach was a deciding factor for the success of blended learning. To realize learner's centric Learning Module was developed in the subsequent way. As clearly from the term Learner centric approach, this task purpose was to know if the course was being understood, responded and through results given feedback by the students. To appraise the course Ecommerce if it was a learner's centric following measures were given such as Start here, Syllabus, Assignment, Lectures Notes, Discussion board and Written Examination [15].

Start here: Start here was an action where students got the clear idea about the follow up the whole contents step wise. In simple language we had tried to let learners know the overall structure of the course, with the use of communication tools between students and teachers so that they could be comfortable and how they could clear their doubts and receive navigating clues how to follow the course to meet its goals. We clearly broadcasted on the Announcement tool for Start here tool and other Navigating details on the Announcement tool also clear details about communication mode between students and teacher had been filed [16].

Syllabus: Syllabus was a detailed description of all the components of the course, for Ecommerce syllabus, clear inclusive about all the minute details to the students were given. Comprehensive syllabus was uploaded on the start here tool, with course contents so that students can easily access to the course guide lines [16].

Assignment: For the course Ecommerce two assignments as case studies were given to the students, they were asked to submit individually on the assignment tool as well as send through course mail. These assignments were given to the students according to the learning outcomes on the topic concerned and therefore uploaded after the completion of the particular topic. Considering the learner's approach, for crystal clear communication all assignment details with pre- requisites were uploaded on announcement tool for the student's information [16].

Lecture Notes: Ecommerce course was a blended course then full online, therefore Prior to the lectures handouts were given to the students and content types was uploaded on lecture tools as usual rule availability of lectures notes and details of conducting lectures be it on line or traditional were declared on announcement tool. For every chapter students were given lectures as a content type PPT, Web Pages, simulated case studies.

Discussion Board: Discussion board was a tool where students got an opportunity to express their opinions, expressions, feedback and creativity as well as critical analytical skills. In consideration to learner's centric approach students were asked to create individual discussion thread on reasoning based issues related to the learning objectives of the respective topics [18]. Students successfully responded on the discussion board and got motivated students in persuasion of the course.

Examination [19, 20]: Ecommerce has practical as well as theory topics and grades distribution changed when the course transformed from face to face to virtual learning. Both types of learning were conducted on LMS e-exam tool but usual pattern of question paper was made consisting the sections such as Objective questions like Fill in the Blanks, True and false, wrong statements needed to be rectified, Identify the term from its Definition, Identify the Differentiation of terms, Analytical and reasoning based objective questions, so that all learning domains are covered.

Feedback: For the success of any efforts feedback process was a vital concern, regular follow up was made as responsible teachers for all the students understanding traditionally on face to face interaction, answering on office telephone, meeting students during their official contact hours in office as well as through answering personal e-mail [21-23].

Summary: To make Ecommerce course as learners centric we tried to put strict and flexible methodology for students on different activities as required to result in good understanding for the subject matter which could cope with upcoming challenges.

In Sample Assessment [24] side Learning outcomes [25] were structured in Activities and further through Assessment result all the standards got alignment and as a sample chapter eight had been reported. Learning outcomes were appraised on various activities based on assessment methods such as on online assignments, online Discussion Board [26], E- Quiz [26] and Online Final Examination [27, 28]. Based on Activities Assessment methods had been decided therefore students would be assuaged to comprehend and solve each problem chosen under assessment criterion [29].

We tried to grade students in various ways; marks were one option, then giving a complimentary second opening to complete any online activity if they complete any prior activity on time, they could receive a second chance to complete other activity if they couldn't meet the deadline.

4. Results

In the closed ended questionnaire many questions pertaining to technological part were asked. Such as which technological tutorial such as LMS/CMS had been used, which software was used to deliver the course so on, list of questions are given in Table 3 and scaled on likert measurement. This research chapter shows the working for E-Learning for all types of assessments, activities and teaching methods. Results show that there was no variation in learning outcomes before and during COVID. LMS has provided an excellent platform of learning and students were found to be engaged in learning process. Teachers have to work harder to transform all traditional learning to virtual learning; they have to plan the online teaching practices and prepared online assessments to meet learning outcomes. This module in Business management was measured to find the effectiveness of E-learning and applications of QM and the Table given below shows the results of positive impact. This chapter presents the motivation to all the instructors to apply QM and LMS practices in learning and teaching, also students are found to enjoy online learning and submitting online assessments. Although some issues of privacy and other false means were identified and these issues were solved by the instructors through applying restrictive measures on assessment completion.

Table 3. Likert scale measurement for learning module Ecommerce

Questions	Highly Functional	Moderately Functional	Neither Functional nor not Functional	Moderately Not Functional	Not Functional at all
To what extent the online components were effective?	5	4	3	2	1
To what extent the course objective were met?	5	4	3	2	1
To what extent the syllabus development was effective?	5	4	3	2	1
To what extent this material was effective to meet learning objective for the module?	5	4	3	2	1
To what extent Audio and Visual components were effective?	5	4	3	2	1
To what extent Quality Rubircs were applied in the course?	5	4	3	2	1

Conclusion

This research focus on the application of QM models in EL but also briefly explains the relevance of EL in achieving economies of scale for any academy particularly for this public university. EL facilitates the academy to impart education to students at large, focus global H.E. and make optimum use of IT in educational sector apart from this these benefits also facilitate in providing effective teaching pedagogy to instructors in all disciplines. This study clearly defined that the Reference Model of Quality Matters for E- Learning standards can be applied for all types of Modules and specifically for Blended courses in the learning paradigm. Also this study magnifies the patterns how QM standards facilitate E-Learning in PU. Through assessments results, online instructors were able to measure the course learning outcomes. It was found that the application of Quality Matters standards facilitated in enhancing online learning environment. This Case study provided a structural format for all the discipline to follow and achieve CLO. This is a case study based on learning and teaching using online mode; application of Quality matters QM in meeting course learning outcomes. Same strategies can be applied in any theoretical or practical modules using various assessment methods. These theoretical or practical courses under any discipline can be fully online, blended with different percentages like 30% online 70% traditional, 50% for each online and traditional, 70% online and 30% traditional, fully traditional course. All the types of courses can apply general rubrics of QM and specific rubrics based on the online percentage and eventually if the QM rubrics are successfully applied the course will meet its learning outcomes.

References

[1] Raza, S. A., Qazi, W., Khan, K. A., & Salam, J. (2021). Social isolation and acceptance of the learning management system (LMS) in the time of COVID-19 pandemic: an expansion of the UTAUT model. *Journal of Educational Computing Research*, *59*(2), 183-208.

[2] Cochran-Smith, M. (2003). *Teaching quality matters.*

[3] Matters, Q. (2016). *About quality matters.*

[4] Nicholson, P. (2007). *A history of e-learning. In Computers and education* (pp. 1-11). Springer, Dordrecht.

[5] Naim, A., & Alahmari, F. (2020). Reference model of e-learning and quality to establish interoperability in higher education systems. *International Journal of Emerging Technologies in Learning (iJET),* 15(2), 15-28.

[6] Almaiah, M. A., Al-Khasawneh, A., & Althunibat, A. (2020). Exploring the critical challenges and factors influencing the E-learning system usage during COVID-19 pandemic. *Education and Information Technologies*, *25*, 5261-5280.

[7] Naim, A., Hussain, M. R., Naveed, Q. N., Ahmad, N., Qamar, S., Khan, N., & Hweij, T. A. (2019, April). Ensuring interoperability of e-learning and quality development in education. In *2019 IEEE Jordan International Joint Conference on Electrical Engineering and Information Technology (JEEIT)* (pp. 736-741). IEEE.

[8] Radha, R., Mahalakshmi, K., Kumar, V. S., & Saravanakumar, A. R. (2020). E-Learning during lockdown of COVID-19 pandemic: A global perspective. *International journal of control and automation*, *13*(4), 1088-1099.

[9] Arshi Naim. (2020). Realization of diverse Electronic tools in learning and teaching for students with diverse skills. *Global Journal of Enterprise Information System*, 12(1), 72-78. Retrieved from https://www.gjeis.com/index.php/GJEIS/article/view/451.

[10] Alqahtani, A. Y., & Rajkhan, A. A. (2020). E-learning critical success factors during the COVID-19 pandemic: A comprehensive analysis of e-learning managerial perspectives. *Education sciences*, *10*(9), 216.

[11] Ellis, R. A., Ginns, P., & Piggott, L. (2009). E-learning in higher education: some key aspects and their relationship to approaches to study. *Higher Education Research & Development*, 28(3), 303-318.

[12] Naim, A. (2018). Strategies to Achieve Students' Centric Approach in Blended Learning. *International Journal of Engineering and Management Research (IJEMR),* 8(2), 214-219.

[13] Cochran-Smith, M. (2003). Teaching quality matters.

[14] Legon, R. (2015). Measuring the impact of the Quality Matters Rubric™: A discussion of possibilities. *American Journal of Distance Education,* 29(3), 166-173.

[15] Naim, A., Sattar, R. A., Al Ahmary, N.., & Razwi, M. T. (2021) *Implementation of Quality Matters Standards on Blended Courses: A Case Study.* FINANCE INDIA Indian Institute of Finance Vol. XXXV No. 3, September 2021 Pages—873 – 890.

[16] Ebner, M., Schön, S., Braun, C., Ebner, M., Grigoriadis, Y., Haas, M., & Taraghi, B. (2020). COVID-19 epidemic as E-learning boost? Chronological development and effects at an Austrian university against the background of the concept of "E-Learning Readiness." *Future Internet*, *12*(6), 94.

[17] Naim, A. (2021). Application of Quality Matters in Digital Learning in Higher Education. *Texas Journal of Multidisciplinary* Studies, 1(1), 3-12.

[18] Legon, R. (2006). Comparison of the quality matters rubric to accreditation standards for distance learning. Retrieved September, 14, 2011.

[19] Lowenthal, P. R., & Hodges, C. B. (2015). In search of quality: Using quality matters to analyze the quality of massive, open, online courses (MOOCs). *International Review of Research in Open and Distributed Learning*, 16(5), 83-101.

[20] Gregory, R. L., Rockinson-Szapkiw, A. J., & Cook, V. S. (2020). Community College Faculty Perceptions of the Quality Matters™ Rubric. *Online Learning*, 24(2), 128-141.

[21] Hollowell, G. P., Brooks, R. M., & Anderson, Y. B. (2017). Course design, quality matters training, and student outcomes. *American Journal of Distance Education*, 31(3), 207-216.

[22] Yusuf, N., & Al-Banawi, N. (2013). The impact of changing technology: The case of e-learning. *Contemporary Issues in Education Research (CIER),* 6(2), 173-180.

[23] Morris, D. (2008). Economies of scale and scope in e-learning. *Studies in higher education*, 33(3), 331-343.

[24] Rodgers, T. (2008). Student engagement in the e-learning process and the impact on their grades. *International Journal of Cyber Society and Education,* 1(2), 143-156.

[25] Naim, A., Khan, M. F., Hussain, M. R., & Khan, N. (2019). "Virtual Doctor" Management Technique in the Diagnosis of ENT Diseases. *JOE,* 15(9), 88.

[26] Mseleku, Z. (2020). A literature review of E-learning and E-teaching in the era of COVID-19 pandemic. *SAGE*, *57*(52), 588-597.

[27] Naim, A., Alahmari, F., & Rahim, A. (2021). Role of Artificial Intelligence in Market Development and Vehicular Communication. *Smart Antennas: Recent Trends in Design and Applications,* 2, 28.

[28] Mahmood, S. (2021). Instructional strategies for online teaching in COVID-19 pandemic. *Human Behavior and Emerging Technologies*, *3*(1), 199-203.

[29] Kaup, S., Jain, R., Shivalli, S., Pandey, S., & Kaup, S. (2020). Sustaining academics during COVID-19 pandemic: the role of online teaching-learning. *Indian Journal of Ophthalmology*, *68*(6), 1220.

Chapter 7

Application of Data Management System in Business-to-Business Electronic Commerce

Shad Ahmad Khan[1,*], Hesham Magd[2] and Ferdinand J. Epoc[1]
[1]College of Business, University of Buraimi, Al Buraimi, Oman
[2]Faculty of Business & Economics, Modern College of Business and Science, Al Buraimi, Oman

Abstract

E-commerce (EC) is a popular term also occasionally known as Internet Commerce which has grown drastically in the past few decades. Covid 19 has made most of the firms to consider EC as a necessity. At one place EC has started to grow and Business to Business Electronic Commerce (B2BEC) too has been implemented by many businesses. The process includes the transaction of goods and services, the transfer of funds and the exchange of data virtually. B2BEC opens up new possibilities of trade and for new business partners from around the globe can be found, their offers can be compared, even complex negotiations can be conducted electronically, and a contract can be drawn up and fulfilled via an electronic marketplace. However, sophisticated data management is required to provide such facilities. On the other hand the contribution of the researchers cannot be ignored in the present context, as they bring on surface many pertinent issues and potential solutions with regard to the daily problems faced by the society. The researchers also are responsible

* Corresponding Author's Email: khan.shadahmad@gmail.com.

In: Competitive Trends and Technologies in Business Management
Editors: Arshi Naim and Praveen K. Malik
ISBN: 978-1-68507-612-2

for unearthing issues that might become a point of concern in the future. The researchers' works need to be reviewed in a systematic way so as to identify the gaps where the future research can be conducted and the gaps can be filled. As the database management is increasingly having relevance in the arena of B2BEC, it is crucial to check the holistic retrospective in this study in light of literature available. As there are no review papers till date in the arena of database management in B2BEC, the present paper is dedicated to explore for the same and propose gaps identified in this area. For this purpose, the paper adopts bibliometric analysis of SCOPUS database i.e., the largest database for scientific studies.

1. Introduction

As the world is changing and quickly adopting the digital environment, the way businesses buy and sell their offerings is also dramatically changing. E-commerce (EC) as a term and practice has gained popularity like never before. Online platforms for almost all the activities have seen a robust boom due to Covid 19. Today the firms have started marking their online presence, and are trying to harness the digital workspace for their different activities. With the growth of EC there has been a substantial growth in Business-to-Business Electronic Commerce (B2BEC) as well. Many businesses are considering this now as a necessity, the regular business processes like the transaction of goods and services, the transfer of funds and the exchange of data etc., have been shifted to the digital platforms. B2BEC has brought up many opportunities in terms of trade and new business partners across the globe. With an increase in the EC, there has been an increasing need for database management as well. Database management helps e-commerce retailers and business owners to serve their customers better by streamlining their processes. The database captures important information that can be utilized by the companies for various purposes. In the online world, information management is the key to success and may at times require companies to embrace software that can take care of this responsibility in a better way and can save time, money and stress for the web-based companies.

As researchers, it is important to take in cognizance of this change that is happening around the world, and identify what the academic and research world is doing in this field. The researchers are experienced to bring pertinent issues and provide solutions to the problems. As digital technology is changing at a faster pace, the academic world is also expected to be abreast with all such changes. This paper intends to analyse the application of Data Management System in Business-to-Business Electronic Commerce through bibliometric analysis of SCOPUS database i.e., the largest database for scientific studies. The main purpose of this study is to identify the key areas where the studies have been done in the context of database management, e-business, and database management in business-to-business e-commerce. As there are no review papers till date in the arena of database management in B2BEC, the present paper is dedicated to look for the same and propose gaps identified.

2. Literature Review

E-commerce's latest trends, highlighted by the global phenomena of the COVID-19 pandemic, explicitly show substantial changes in the online consumers' behavior as well [13]. E-Commerce or Electronic Commerce means buying and selling of goods, products, or services over the internet. E-commerce is also known as electronic commerce or internet commerce. These services are provided online over the internet network. Transactions of money, funds, and data are also considered as E-commerce. In short, E-commerce is a commercial transaction that has happened over the internet. These business transactions can be done in four ways: Business to Business (B2B), Business to Customer (B2C), Customer to Customer (C2C), and Customer to Business (C2B). The e-business may be seen as an opportunity to make legacy systems evolve in order to be compatible with the new technologies [11]. Business-to-business applications have become increasingly important in recent times. The area of Business-to-Business Electronic Commerce (B2B EC) is expected to grow dramatically in coming years. Database management system (DBMS) is usually a software that provides facilities for managing the data used in various information system (IS) processes. According to Date & Hopewell (1971) and ANSI (1978), The DBMS enables to achieve independence between a program implementing IS process and the physical representation of the data [1, 2]. The DBMS technology has seen various phases referred as generation, starting from using network data [3, 4] to relational data model [5, 6] or the object-oriented one [7, 8, 10] or a mixture of model referred as object-relational data model [9].

Over time, the DBMS technology has evolved to meet the new hardware and software requirements and needs [11]. Rapid development of the e-commerce industry has brought a craze to online shopping. This has led to growth in transaction volume on e-commerce platforms, which has further led to accumulation of large amounts of data [12].

Such data hold a lot of valuable information that can be mined to explore the defects in the product, needs of the consumer, pattern of requirement [12].

The bibliometric analysis involves quantitative tools for analysis of bibliographic information [20]. This approach is very helpful in analyzing the large amount of literature or bibliographic data. The approach of this analysis is objective in nature i.e., number of citations and publications, occurrences of keywords and topics [15, 16].

It helps in deciphering and mapping the cumulative scientific knowledge and evolutionary nuances of established fields of study. The benefits involve providing one stop overview of the literature, identifying knowledge gaps, deriving novelty of ideas or investigation, and positioning their intended contributions to the field [15]. The bibliometric analysis has been proven to be applied in different disciplines of business research [16, 19], also electronic commerce [18], & Digital Entrepreneurship [17]. The bibliometric analysis has a variety of approaches that includes studying publications, collaborative partners, countries associated in research, intellectual structure of the research field [15, 16]. It can also check the trends and approach of specific journals or specific fields over a period of time.

The bibliometric methods have been found to be appropriate to provide retrospectives of the literature available in specific fields or of journals [15, 16].

3. Methodology

Bibliometric methodology has been used in the paper that involves quantitative tools for the analysis of literature i.e., bibliographic information [20].

For this purpose, the csv files were downloaded from the Scopus website, the largest database of scientific documents using the key words "Business to Business" AND "E Commerce"; "Database Management"; "Database management AND E-Commerce AND Business to Business". The generated files were uploaded into Vos viewer to check the Co-Occurrence of all key words to extract the most popular words in the domain, country analysis has been done to check the national background of the authors, and citations analysis has been conducted to check the strength of the document as per the standard recommendations of Donthu et al., (2021) and Khan et al., (2021)

[16, 17]. The main objective of the study is to identify the gaps in literature through the following specific objectives:

1. To check the number of documents in the domain of database management in B2BEC.
2. To check the top contributing countries in the proposed arena.
3. To identify the cluster of prominent keywords utilized in the studies.

4. Analysis and Findings through Bibliometric Analysis

4.1. Database Management

As a starting point of the study, it was important to find out the current trends in Database management, and check the visibility of business-related content in the Scopus database [15, 16]. A total of 2001 documents were found in the Scopus database with the keyword "database management*".

It is crucial for the study to check the orientation of the research available in the field. Since the database is big, the researchers attempted to check the most prominent words or topics covered in the study in the field of database management and relate its presence in the business and commerce-based studies. In order to increase the coverage of the keywords, the co-occurrence was set at 30 and above. A total of 36 items were extracted through this filter, the highlights of the same are captured in Table 1 below.

The studies in database management, have been concentrated in the areas majorly as Database management system (s); Human(s); Information management; Database system; Query processing; Article; Management information systems; Relational database system; Relational database; management system; Digital storage etc.

Since the business-related terminologies were not found among the top 36 keywords, the researchers explored the complete list of the database and extracted the keywords related to business along with its total link strength as given in Table 2.

It is evident from Tables 1 and 2, that commerce and business have not been significantly represented in the studies related to database management.

This leads to suggest that enough room is available for the future researchers to perform studies in this arena and explore the possibilities to a greater extent.

Table 1. Co-occurrence analysis of database management

S. No	Items	Occurrences	Total link strength
1	Database management system (s)	719	5423
2	Human(s)	655	5152
3	Information management	612	2051
4	Database system	467	1166
5	Query processing	359	1274
6	Article	269	2086
7	Management information systems	255	978
8	Relational database system	247	1004
9	Relational database management system	237	929
10	Digital storage	200	866
11	Factual database	178	1718
12	Query Languages	178	681
13	Big data	162	765
14	Procedures	157	1443
15	Data handling	129	558
16	Priority journal	127	1101
17	Software	120	1012
18	Information processing	109	966
19	Search engine (s)	104	547
20	Data mining	98	551
21	Female	83	740
22	Information retrieval	80	748
23	Male	78	706
24	Semantics	75	646
25	Controlled study	72	605
26	Internet	67	624
27	Adult	66	602
28	Genetics	56	491
29	Biology	55	556
30	Computer interface	54	562
31	Computational biology	51	526
32	Information storage and retrieval	50	532
33	Internet of Things	45	409
34	User-computer interface	43	477
35	Algorithm	31	506
36	Website	31	298

Source: Extracted from scopus.com via Vos Viewer (authors calculation).

Table 2. Other important keywords related to business not covered under Table 1

S. No	Keywords	Occurrences	Total link strength
1	Data Collection	23	329
2	Economic and Social Effect	21	141
3	Mobile application	17	297
4	Block chain	16	109
5	Decision trees	13	106
6	Life cycle	12	81
7	Managers	11	81
8	Resource Management	10	73
9	Human Resource Management	9	79
10	Database performance	9	81
11	Social Networking	9	86
12	Decision support system	9	97
13	Taxonomies	8	81
14	Multivariate analysis	7	143
15	Research and development	6	52
16	Management	6	77
17	Pandemic	6	82
18	Feedback system	6	94
19	Cross Sectional Studies	6	126
20	Manufacture	5	30

Source: Extracted from scopus.com via Vos Viewer (authors calculation).

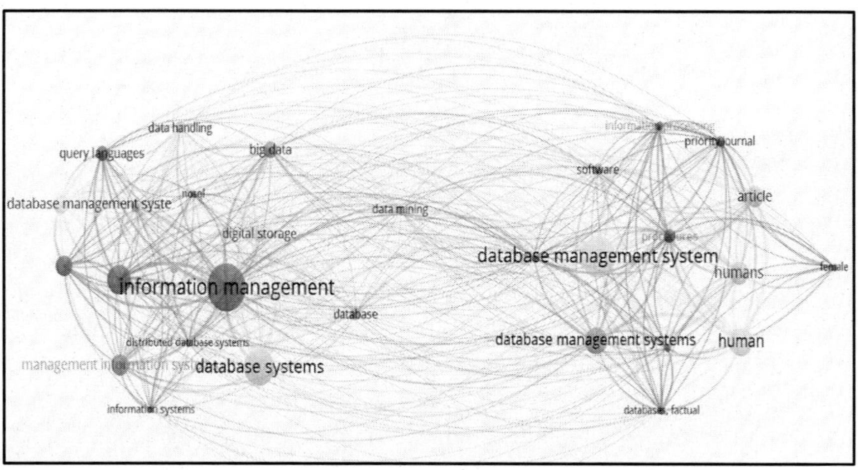

Figure 1. Bibliometric graph- database management (showing the links and network of the studies) (Source: Extracted from scopus.com via Vos Viewer (authors calculation)).

However, if the research in the arena of database management systems can be grouped, the bibliometric graph as given under Figure 1, suggest that the documents can be divided into two major clusters i.e., cluster 1: database management system; and cluster 2: management information system.

Country wise co-authorship analysis suggests the involvement of countries in the given field [15]. Total 144 countries were found to be involved in the studies in the arena of Database management out of which top 15 as represented in Figure 2, the highest contribution in the field of database management is found for the United States followed by China, Germany, United Kingdom and India.

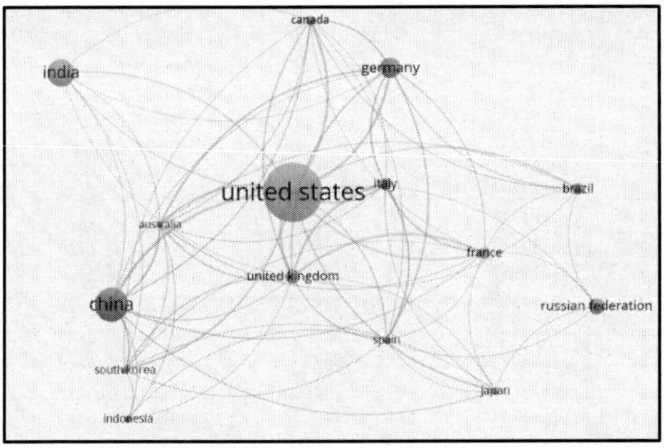

Figure 2. Bibliometric graph- database management (country wise studies) (Source: Extracted from scopus.com via Vos Viewer (authors' calculation)).

4.2. Electronic Commerce

The bibliometric analysis was also performed for the electronic commerce to understand the trends and major concentration topics.

Top 10 items were explored from the Scopus database using the keyword as "electronic commerce" AND "E-Commerce" as given under Table 3.

Figure 2, represents the cluster analysis of the major items covered in the studies around E-commerce. The prominent items as visible in the Figure 3 are internet of things; mobile commerce; information management; big data; decision making; behavioral research; websites; profitability; marketing etc. The database management or database management system however, could not make its prominent position in the bibliometric graph suggesting a big gap in the literature around e-commerce.

Table 3. Co-Occurrence analysis of electronic commerce

S. No	Items	Occurrences	Total link strength
1	Electronic Commerce	1115	2431
2	Sales	296	916
3	E Commerce	538	1184
4	Recommender system	111	308
5	Decision making	99	300
6	Deep learning	76	259
7	Online shopping	86	257
8	Machine Learning	82	252
9	Website	79	248
10	Consumer behaviour	73	241

Source: Extracted from scopus.com via Vos Viewer (authors calculation).

Country wise, authors from 133 countries have contributed in the field of electronic commerce as listed in the Scopus database that is less than the number of countries conducting research in the arena of database management.

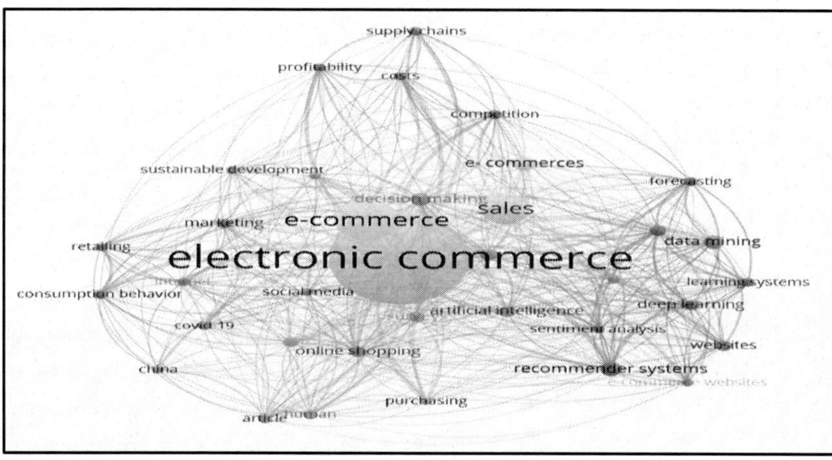

Figure 3. Bibliometric graph- E-Commerce (showing the links and network of the studies) (Source: Extracted from scopus.com via Vos Viewer (authors calculation)).

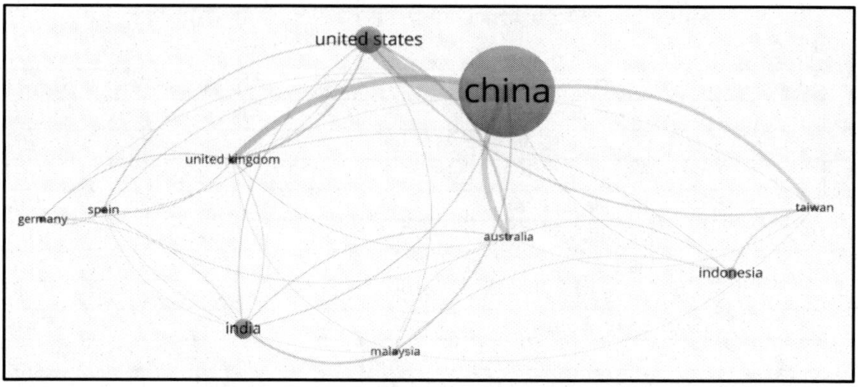

Figure 4. Bibliometric graph- E-commerce (country wise studies) (Source: Extracted from scopus.com via Vos Viewer (authors calculation)).

However, the highest contribution in the field of e-commerce is from China as presented under Figure 4.

4.3. Database Management in B2B E-Commerce

In order to have a specific approach and achieve the objectives of this study.

The keyword used to extract this data from "Database Management*" AND "Business to Business" AND "B2B" AND "E-Commerce" AND "Electronic Commerce". The co-occurrence analysis was performed keeping the minimum threshold of 7 occurrences to expand the coverage of the items. Table 4 and Figure 5 represent the same.

As visible from the Table 4 and Figure 5, the prominent items are electronic commerce; Database systems; e-commerce; Information management; commerce; Internet; Distributed database system; Information systems; xml; Artificial intelligence; Data mining; Web services. A total of 46 countries were found active in this field out of which only 14 countries have 4 or more documents in the scopus database. The co-author analysis of these countries is given as under Figure 6.

It is observable from the figure, the highest amount of work has been done from the United States, followed by China, Australia, Taiwan and Canada. Cluster Analysis helps the researchers to find the combination of items used in one or more studies that establishes the major types of studies done in the broad area [15]. In total 5 such clusters of work were identified in the arena of database management in B2BEC as presented in Table 5.

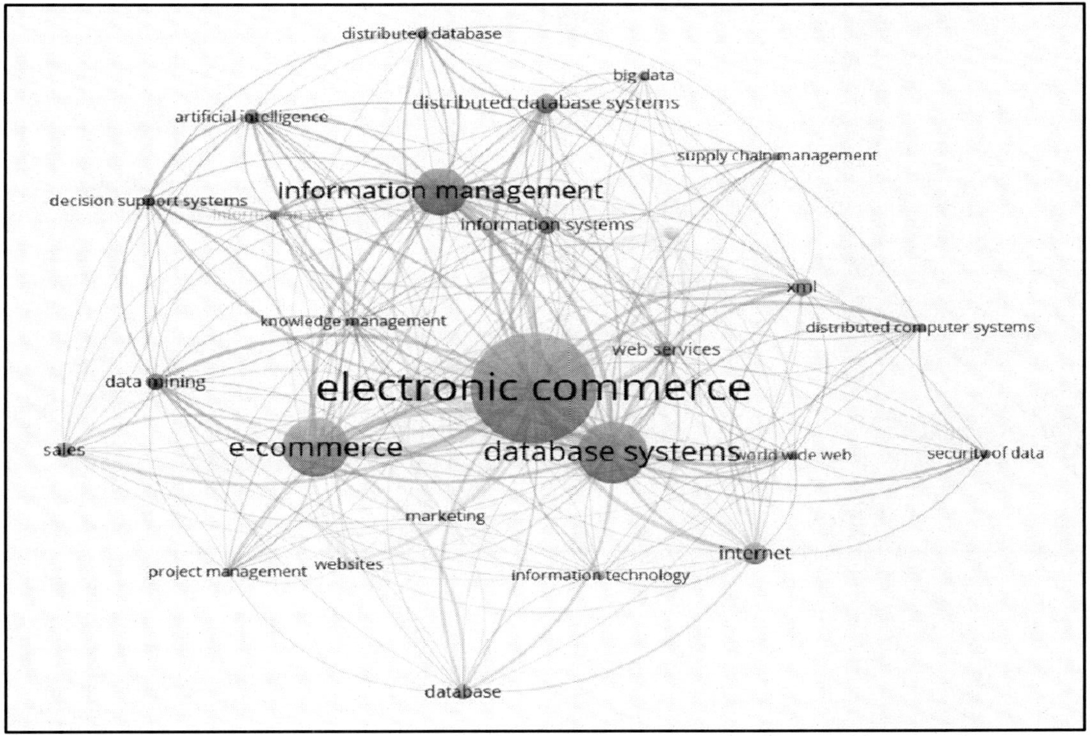

Figure 5. Bibliometric Graph-Database management in B2B E-Commerce (showing the links and network of the studies) (Source: Extracted from scopus.com via Vos Viewer (authors calculation)).

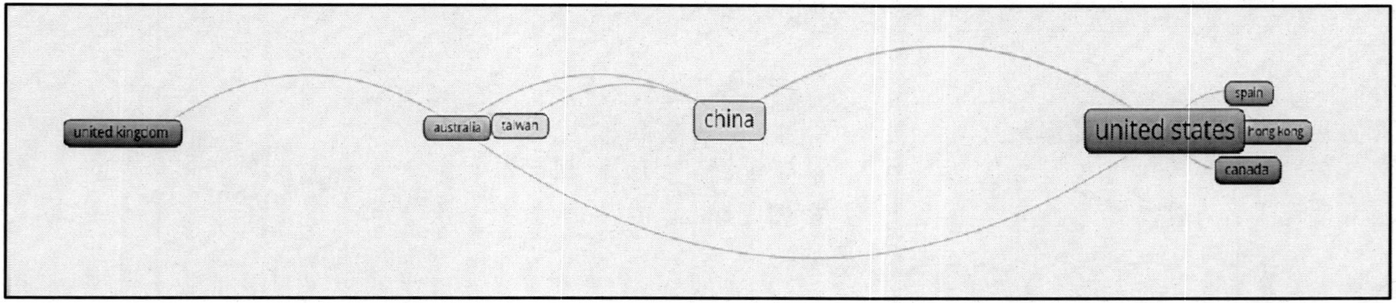

Figure 6. Bibliometric Graph-Database management in B2B E-Commerce **(country wise)** (Source: Extracted from scopus.com via Vos Viewer (authors calculation)).

Table 4. Co-occurrence analysis of database management in B2B e-commerce

S. No	Items	Occurrences	Total link strength
1	Electronic commerce	86	257
2	Database systems	48	160
3	e-commerce	46	145
4	Information management	37	119
5	Commerce	16	69
6	Internet	17	56
7	Distributed database system	15	53
8	Information systems	14	49
9	Xml	14	48
10	Artificial intelligence	11	47
11	Data mining	13	43
12	Web services	12	42
13	Management information system	11	41
14	Database	12	38
15	Decision support systems	9	38
16	Marketing	9	37
17	Distributed database	9	34
18	Sales	12	33
19	World wide web	8	31
20	Information use	7	27
21	Websites	9	30
22	Project management	7	27
23	Knowledge management	7	25
24	Distributed computer systems	7	24
25	Information technology	8	24
26	Security data	7	20
27	Supply chain management	7	18
28	Big data	8	16

Source: Extracted from scopus.com via Vos Viewer (authors calculation).

Table 5. Cluster analysis of database management in B2B e-commerce

Cluster 1 (8 items)				
Big data	**Cluster 2 (8 items)**			
Distributed data	Database systems	**Cluster 3 (7 items)**		
Distributed database system	Distributed computer system	Commerce	**Cluster 4 (4 items)**	
Information management system	Electronic commerce	Database	Artificial intelligence	**Cluster 5 (1 items)**
Information system	Internet	e-commerce	Data mining	websites
Information use	Management information systems	Information technology	Decision support system	
Supply chain management	Security of data	Marketing	Knowledge management	
Webservices	World wide web	Project management		
	Xml	sales		

Source: Extracted from scopus.com via Vos Viewer (authors calculation).

Conclusion and Recommendations

The findings of the bibliometric analysis signifies that there is a big gap in terms of the research done in the field of database management systems in B2B e-commerce. As the need for database management is increasingly felt in the domain of e-business and e-commerce. The research attention is also needed to be drawn in this arena. The total number of countries active in the present field was found to be only 46, i.e., less than 1/3 of the countries active in doing research in the field of database management. The internet boom that has happened due to covid 19, might have increased the dominance of e-commerce. On the other hand, database management and information systems being very old concepts have been researched more. However, the inter-connection of database management with the business world was found to be missing as per the findings of this study. In total, all the objectives set for the study have been met.

The area of database management systems in B2B e-commerce is found to be less researched, and more contextual studies are recommended in the future.

References

[1] ANSI/X3/SPARC Study Group on Data Base Management Systems (1978). Framework report on database management systems, *Information Systems,* 3(3), pp. 173 - 191.

[2] Date, C. J. and Hopewell, P. (1971). File definition and Logical Data Independence, *ACM SIGFIDET Workshop on Data Description, Access and Control,* ACM Ed., New York.

[3] Bachman, C. (1969). Data structure diagrams, *Journal of Association of Computing Machinery (ACM),* Special Interest Group on Business Data Processing (The current name of this journal is DATABASE) 1, (2), pp. 4 - 10.

[4] Taylor, R. W. and Frank, R. L. (1976). Codasyl Data Base Management Systems, *ACM Computing Surveys*, 8(1), pp. 67 - 103.

[5] Codd, E. F. (1970). A relational model for large shared data banks, *ACM Communications*, 13, (6), pp. 377 - 387.

[6] Astrahan, M., Blasgen, M., Chamberlin, D., Eswaran, K., Gray, J., Griffiths, P., King, W., Lorie, R., McJones, P., Mehl J., Putzolu, G., Traiger, I., Wade, B. and Watson, V. (1976). System R: Relational approach to database management, *ACM Transactions on Database Systems,* 1, (2), pp. 97 - 137.

[7] Atkinson, M., Bancilhon, F., DeWitt, D., Dittrich, K., Maier, D. and Zdonik, S. (1989). The Object- Oriented Database System Manifesto, *Deductive and Object-Oriented Databases International Conference,* Kyoto, Japan.

[8] Bancilhon, F., Delobel, C. and Kanellakis, P. (1992). *Building an Object-Oriented Database System: The Story of O2* (San Francisco, CA, Morgan Kaufmann Pub.).

[9] Stonebraker, M. and Moore, D. (1996). *Object-Relational DBMSs: The Next Great Wave* (San Francisco, CA, Morgan Kaufmann Pub.).

[10] Cattel, R. G. G., Barry, D., Bartels, D., Berler, M., Eastman, J., Gammerman, S., Jordan, D., Springer, A., Strickland, H. and Wade, D. (1992). *Object-Oriented Database Standard: ODMG 2.0* (San Francisco, CA Morgan Kaufmann Pub.).

[11] Bouneffa, M., Basson, H. and Deruelle, L. (2010). E-business: A New Challenge for Database Management Systems. *Information &*

Communications Technology Law, 10:3, 299 - 308, DOI: 10.1080/ 13600830120081926.

[12] Yan, B., Wu, C., Yu, R., Yu, B., Shi, N., Zhou, X., Yu, Y. (2021). Big Data-Based E-Commerce Transaction Information Collection Method. *Complexity,* DOI: 10.1155/2021/8665621.

[13] Paştiu, C. A., Oncioiu, I., Gârdan, D. A., Maican, S. Ş., Gârdan, I. P., Muntean, A. C. (2020). The perspective of e-business sustainability and website accessibility of online stores. *Sustainability,* (Switzerland), 12(22). DOI: 10.3390/su12229780.

[14] Lahkani, Marjaneh J., Shouyang Wang, Mariusz Urbański and Mariya Egorova. (2020). "Sustainable B2B E-Commerce and Blockchain-Based Supply Chain Finance". *Sustainability,* 12, no. 10: 3968. https://doi.org/10.3390/su12103968.

[15] Donthu, N., Kumar, S., Mukherjee, D., Pandey, N., Lim, W. M., (2021). How to conduct a bibliometric analysis: An overview and guidelines. *Journal of Business Research*, 133, pp. 285 - 296. https:// doi.org/10.1016/j.jbusres.2021.04.070.

[16] Khan, M. A., Patnaik, D., Ashraf, R., Ali, I., Kumar, S., Donthu, N. (2021). Value of special issues in the Journal of Business Research: A bibliometric analysis. *Journal of Business Research*, 125 (2021), pp. 295 - 313.

[17] Purnomo, A., Susanti, T., Sari, A. K., Firdaus, M. and Dewi, R. (2020). A Study of Digital Entrepreneurship through Bibliometric Visualizing from 1993 to 2019. *International Conference on Information Management and Technology (ICIMTech),* pp. 911 - 915, doi: 10.1109/ICIMTech50083.2020.9211270.

[18] Kumar, S., Lim, W. M., Pandey, N., Westland, J. C. (2021). 20 years of Electronic Commerce Research. *Electronic Commerce Research,* 21 (1), pp. 1 - 40.

[19] Kumar, S., Surekha, R., Lim, W. M., Mangla, S. K. and Goyal, N. (2021). What do we know about business strategy and environmental research? Insights from Business Strategy and the Environment. *Business Strategy and the Environment.* Available at doi: https:// doi.org/10.1002/bse.2813 (in press).

[20] Pritchard, A. (1969). Statistical bibliography or bibliometrics. *Journal of documentation*, 25(4), 348 - 349.

Chapter 8

Applications of E-Learning Tools for Achieving Students Learning Outcomes for Business Programs

Arshi Naim*

Department of Information Systems,
King Khalid University, Abha, Kingdom of Saudi Arabia (KSA)

Abstract

This is an extended research presenting how applications of E-Learning tools aided in meeting the students' learning outcomes and how students with different understanding and cognitive skills can get benefits from E-Learning tools. The current research has tried to find the effectiveness of electronic tool for diverse skills of students. This research confers the suggestions on how Electronic tools in learning management services could be implemented by the instructors in the process of Learning and Teaching (LT) to meet the requirements of different learners in Business Information Systems (BIS). In this study the module chosen was Business Information Systems in Information System's environment. Thurstone scale is used to measure the effectiveness of various electronic tools available on Learning Management Services (LMS) "Blackboard." This paper, we have compared these electronic tools for their effectiveness in meeting learning outcomes for different learners in BIS. For measuring assessments' results, three tools were used namely

* Corresponding Author's Email: arshi@kku.edu.sa.

In: Competitive Trends and Technologies in Business Management
Editors: Arshi Naim and Praveen K. Malik
ISBN: 978-1-68507-612-2

Electronic-Quiz (EQ), Discussion Forum (DF) and Safe Assignment (SA). The paper has tried to measure the effectiveness of a new tool introduced on Blackboard named as Safe Assignment for submitting the assignment. Through this tool instructors were able to identify the percentage of plagiarism or matching between the peers. Based on three assessments' results namely EQ, DF and SA, samples were categorized under best, average and poor. These assessments were considered for the purpose of study because they were conducted by the implementation on electronic tools on LMS. The performance of student in each group was analyzed and it was found that students in all the groups could contribute and learn the best through DF. Best Students tried to learn equally through all the tools but other two groups planted least efforts and submitted their assignments using search engines such as Google.

Keywords: electronic tool, LMS, blackboard, electronic quiz, discussion forum, safe assignment

1. Introduction

King Khalid University (KKU) conveys home learning and worldwide learning openings on campus for male and female students. KKU is in the Kingdom of Saudi Arabia (KSA) and is one of the leading educational centers in the Middle East [4]. In 2008, KKU introduced Blackboard Collaborate TM (BBCl) to accomplish regional and global education and instructional fineness along with effective stipulation of their gender-divided campus for more than 65,000 students, half of which are women [4, 6] through EL on LMS. King Khalid University (KKU) is located in the city of Abha, in the Asir region of the KSA. It is straddling 81,000 square KMs; the university is comprised of 26 different campuses and 48 colleges, offering further and higher education to its students. The university was formed in 1998 from the merger of King Saud and Imam Muhammad Ibn Saud Islamic universities. It introduced an EL centre in 2005 and presently provides courses on an assortment of subjects, including medicine, pharmacy, computer sciences, engineering, Islamic studies, dentistry and education [4-6].

The University has met many challenges like meeting the planned ambition of KKU for female and male students because previously, the university operated separate campuses for male and female students [5]. Male instructors were not able to teach female students in face-to-face environments and formerly used studios where instructors gave lectures to female students who were watching through a television screen in the room next door. Female students were only permitted to ask questions through a telephone attached to the wall. This approach was prohibitive due to many factors including the cost and maintenance of the studios and the university was resolute to develop a more practical and sustainable elucidation [4-6].

Women also faced an additional challenge when it came to travelling for the lectures as a cultural hindrance but now they are not allowed to drive since 2015. Before this time female students at KKU were dependent on their male relatives for commuting for lectures and other academic activities. This was a huge barricade to education; similarly disabled students also faced travelling challenges due to cost and their limitations.

2. Literature Review

A feature that is particularly relevant to KKU's gender separated population is the ability to provide instantaneous collaboration through the operation of instant messaging on BBCl enterprise [4, 6]. This has enabled students and teachers to work together in an informal "virtual environment," therefore they are able to chat, connect through video to have one-to-one interviews, and share their desktops with one another to exchange ideas and all these methods enhance the communication in all the perspectives [4-6].

In 2005, the university established its first EL centre and in 2008, chose BBCl to integrate with the university's primary LMS, Blackboard Learn™. Mohammad Qatrawi, Research and Development Manager at the EL Center at KKU state "Choosing online collaboration was a strategic decision [4-6]." It provides equal chances for all, quality, and better student experiences and keeps us up to date with best practices [4, 5]. So, BBCl was used to support achieving EL vision [4]."

With this idea on education, many of the facet and capabilities of the BBCl™ online collaboration platform are assisting KKU with its EL vision. Most widely used capabilities are web conferencing for hosting virtual classrooms, the whiteboard for making classes more engaging and interactive, polling for answering questions, and instant messaging [4-6].

Over 7,000 students across 25 departments, including medicine, pharmacy, dentistry, computer sciences, engineering, education, Sharia and religion, training, and more are adopting online collaboration into their prospectus today [6].

The increase in adoption has been driven by their 'top-down' vision where instructors are comprehensively trained either face-to-face or online. All of the contents and training materials are published on the university's EL Deanship' website and EL specialists can be reached personally for all EL related assistance [4].

3. Research Methodology

This was a descriptive Study based on qualitative analysis. Assumptions show that the "discussion forum" was the most effective electronic tools for meeting the diverse needs of students in the business modules. BBCl has facilitated instructors to communicate learning materials in various methods like videos, presentations, etc. also assessment methods has been refined and became time effective on Blackboard. The assessments were considered for the purpose of study because they were conducted on the electronic tools of LMS. The performance of student in each group was analyzed and it was found that students in all the groups could contribute and learn the best through open DF. Best Students tried to learn equally through all tools but other two groups planted least efforts and submitted their assignments using search engines such as Google.

4. Discussion and Findings

This study was conducted for the session 2019-2020 first semesters. There were two sections for the course of Business Information Systems having 38 students in total. Based on three assessments' results namely EQ, DF and SA, samples were categorized under best, average and poor. These assessments were considered for the purpose of study because they were conducted by the implementation on electronic tool on LMS and aided in meeting the course learning outcomes (CLO) [8-11]. Also it was important to mention that statistics on usage of electronic tool for the purpose of learning the module was done through tracking student's access to online LMS, attendance and finally assessing the activities submitted by the individual student.

For measuring assessments' results, three tools were used namely Electronic-Quiz (EQ), Discussion Forum (DF) and Safe Assignment (SA).

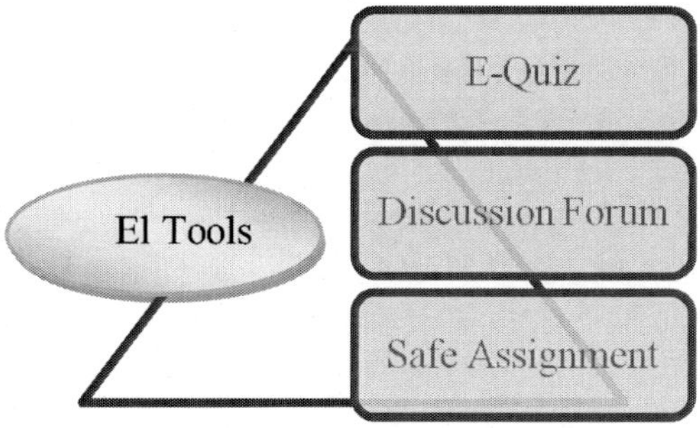

Figure 1. El Tools used on LMS.

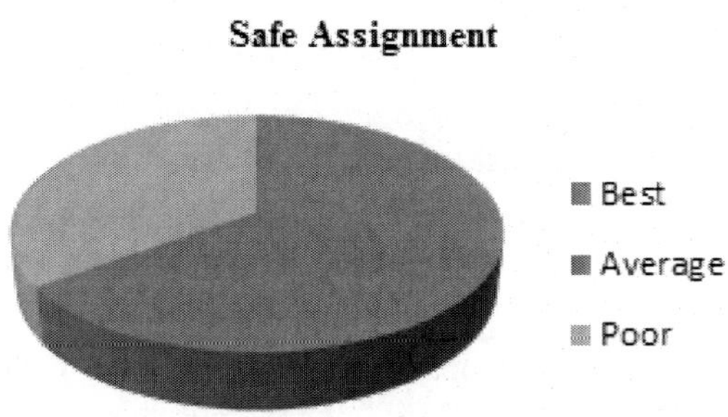

Figure 2. Results of SA for IS module E-Commerce.

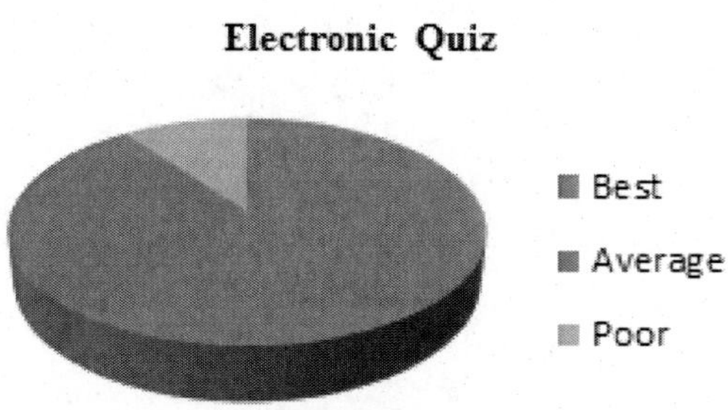

Figure 3. Results of EQ for IS module E-Commerce.

Researchers and course instructors found that SA tool was effective and appropriate to measure the analytical skills of students and this tool helped the researchers to clearly categorize best, average and poor students. This tool was quite effective in identifying the plagiarism too. Results show students are almost equally divided in best, average and poor category. Instructors assume with reference to Quality Matters standards for online learning [1] various activities should be used to meet CLOs for the particular module as learners have diverse skills and needs. Some learners who could not present their ideas in close ended environment but could perform well in opened learning environment. Language barrier and cognitive skills were the main reasons for poor performance for many students. Average students were found to take most of the information from search engines but they tried to explain in their own words too. Best students were excellent in analysis, performed a good research and submitted their assignments in most distinguished manner.

Researchers found that EQs were very effective electronic tools to meet the needs of diverse students' populations to meet learning outcome of the particular module. There were various types of questions presented on EQ like multiple choices, either-or, true and false, fill in the blanks, pools and matching, etc. Some questioned needed manual grading and other types were graded automatically as the answers provided by the instructor were close ended. 60% of the students were graded under the category of best students and only 10% students could not perform very well.

Researchers found that DF was the most effective electronic tools to meet the needs of diverse student populations to meet learning outcome of the particular module. 80% of the learners performed very well and participated in active learning on the forum. Some students also created discussion threads and invited their peers to participate or to write blogs. Only 5% percent of the learners were found not very participative but reasons were not known. Instructors assume that it could be due to language barrier. LMS has helped KKU to conquer many of its challenges around enhancing the quality of education, improving access to teaching and resources, and meeting CLOs. Also this tool helped in developing interpersonal skills amongst the students.

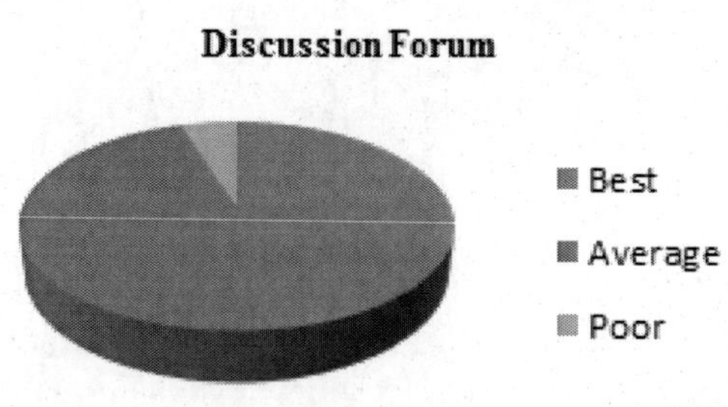

Figure 4. Results of DF for IS module E-Commerce.

Furthermore a short E-Survey was conducted on LMS to know effectiveness of EL tools and techniques. There were 50 respondents, all 38 students from two sections of Business Information Systems module and 12 EL experts/instructors were given this close ended questionnaire. Below given table shows 5 Points Scale from strongly Agree to Strongly Disagree:

Table 1. Result analysis for effectively of EL tools on LMS in KKU

Questions	Strongly Agree	Agree	Neutral	Disagree	Strongly Disagree
Do you think LMS has effective application in Higher Education?	35	10	5	0	0
Do find LMS applications effective in KKU	35	10	5	0	0
Do think Elluninate live is effective medium for course instruction?	35	10	5	0	0
Do you think LMS has solved the problem of Gender divide?	35	10	5	0	0
Do you find LMS effective for Assessment Methods?	35	10	5	0	0
Do you think LMS has Quality services?	35	10	5	0	0
Do you think LMS has solved the problem of online learning for the students commuting from remote areas?	35	10	5	0	0
How would you rate your experience with LMS?	35	10	5	0	0

Respondents were also asked to rate the level of quality [2], of various tools of LMS for KKU on the scale of Excellent to Poor.

Table 2. Result analysis for quality service of LMS tools in KKU

Questions	Excellent	Very Good	Good	Fair	Poor
Elluminate Live	10	20	20	0	0
Trigity Tool	15	20	15	0	0
Assignment	35	15	0	0	0
Content Area	50	0	0	0	0
Assessment Tools	50	0	0	0	0
Course tools	40	6	4	0	0
Communication Tool	25	5	16	4	0

Respondents were asked to rate the frequency of using a particular LMS Blackboard tool in instructing their modules on the scale of Every Time to Never.

Table 3. Result Analysis for frequency of using service of LMS tools [3]

Questions	Every Time	Almost Every Time	Occasionally	Almost Never	Never
Elluminate Live	0	5	45	0	0
Trigity Tool	0	5	45	0	0
Safe Assignment	0	5	45	0	0
Content Area	40	0	10	0	0
Assessment Tools	40	0	10	0	0
Course tools	0	5	45	0	0
Communication Tool	0	5	45	0	0

5. Results

The performance of students in each group was analyzed and it was found that students in all the groups could contribute and learn the best through open discussion forum. Best Students tried to learn equally through all tools but other two groups planted least efforts and through Google search uploaded their work only. Researchers also concluded that many instructors may not be using EL tools and techniques in meeting CLOs but they well realize the advantages of the applications of EL tools in meeting diverse needs. For example in the situation when students coming from remote areas or students who are disable and also in the condition of gender divide, EL is the most effective methods of learning and teaching. In addition, the EL tools on LMS and BBCl are used to integrate with the university's primary LMS and has changed the entire teaching pedagogy and supported the University in achieving its vision.

EL has exploited the best of BBCl capabilities which are web conferencing for hosting virtual classrooms, the whiteboard for making classes more engaging and interactive, polling for answering questions, and instant messaging, etc., but for the purpose of this study we focused only on three important tools,, SA, DF and EQ.

Conclusion

It was found that discussion forum was the most effective electronic tools to meet the needs of diverse student to meet learning outcome for BIS module. BBCl has facilitated instructors to communicate learning materials through various methods like videos, presentations, etc. and has provided easy platform for conducting assessment methods. Some popular assessment methods used by keen instructors are Quizzes, Online exam, Question mark, Assignment, Blog, Discussion forum and Journals.

Now with the help of EL tools on BBCl, access to teaching and resources has become easier, students with diverse skills, competence and needs are learning better and finally it is helping to manage a gender divided in the university.

References

[1] Fink, L. D. (2003). *Creating Significant Learning Experiences: An Integrated Approach to Designing College Courses*. San Francisco: Jossey-Bass.

[2] McTighe, J., & Ferrara, S. (1995). Assessing learning in the classroom. *Journal of Quality Learning*, 5(2), 95-112.

[3] Suskie, L. (2004). Assessing Student Learning: A Common Sense Guide. Bolton MA: Anker Publishing Company, Inc.

[4] Naim, A., Alahmari, F., & Rahim, A. (2021). Role of Artificial Intelligence in Market Development and Vehicular Communication. *Smart Antennas: Recent Trends in Design and Applications*, 2, 28.

[5] Walvoord, B. E. (2004). Assessment Clear and Simple: A Practical Guide for Institutions, Departments, and General Education. San Francisco: Jossey-B.

[6] Angelo, T. A., & Cross, P. (1993). Classroom Assessment Techniques: *A Handbook for College Teachers*.

[7] Cochran-Smith, M. (2003). Teaching quality matters.

[8] Arshi Naim, Raja Abdul Sattar, Nalah Al Ahmary, Mohammad Tehreem Razwi, Implementation of Quality Matters Standards on Blended Courses: A Case Study (2021) Finance India Indian Institute of Finance Vol. XXXV No. 3, September 2021 Pages 873-890.

[9] Matters, Q. (2016). About quality matters.

[10] Nicholson, P. (2007). A history of e-learning. In: *Computers and education* (pp. 1-11). Springer, Dordrecht.

[11] Naim, A., & Alahmari, F. (2020). Reference model of e-learning and quality to establish interoperability in higher education systems. *International Journal of Emerging Technologies in Learning (iJET),* 15(2), 15-28.

[12] Naim, A., Hussain, M. R., Naveed, Q. N., Ahmad, N., Qamar, S., Khan, N., & Hweij, T. A. (2019, April). Ensuring interoperability of e-learning and

quality development in education. In: *2019 IEEE Jordan International Joint Conference on Electrical Engineering and Information Technology (JEEIT)* (pp. 736-741). IEEE.

[13] Arshi Naim. (2020). Realization of diverse Electronic tools in learning and teaching for students with diverse skills. *Global Journal of Enterprise Information System*, 12(1), 72-78. Retrieved from https://www.gjeis.com/index.php/GJEIS/article/view/451.

[14] Naim, A., Khan, M. F., Hussain, M. R., & Khan, N. (2019). "Virtual Doctor" Management Technique in the Diagnosis of ENT Diseases. *JOE*, 15(9), 88.

[15] Naim, A. (2020). Realization of diverse Electronic tools in learning and teaching for students with diverse skills. *Global Journal of Enterprise Information System*, 12(1), 72-78.

[16] Ellis, R. A., Ginns, P., & Piggott, L. (2009). E-learning in higher education: some key aspects and their relationship to approaches to study. *Higher Education Research & Development*, 28(3), 303-318.

[17] Naim, A. (2018). Strategies to Achieve Students' Centric Approach in Blended Learning. *International Journal of Engineering and Management Research (IJEMR),* 8(2), 214-219.

[18] Cochran-Smith, M. (2003). Teaching quality matters.

[19] Legon, R. (2015). Measuring the impact of the Quality Matters Rubric™: A discussion of possibilities. *American Journal of Distance Education*, 29(3), 166-173.

[20] Arshi Naim (2021). Application of Quality Matters in Digital Learning in Higher Education. *Texas Journal of Multidisciplinary Studies,* 1(1), 3-12. Retrieved from https://zienjournals.com/index. php/tjm/article/view/11.

[21] Naim, A., & Bashir, A. (2016). Application of Quality Matters Standards on Supportive and Online Module in Higher Education Program. *Research Revolution*, 5(3), 6-12.

[22] Lowenthal, P. R., & Hodges, C. B. (2015). In search of quality: Using quality matters to analyze the quality of massive, open, online courses (MOOCs). *International Review of Research in Open and Distributed Learning,* 16(5), 83-101.

[23] Gregory, R. L., Rockinson-Szapkiw, A. J., & Cook, V. S. (2020). Community College Faculty Perceptions of the Quality Matters™ Rubric. *Online Learning*, 24(2), 128-141.

[24] Hollowell, G. P., Brooks, R. M., & Anderson, Y. B. (2017). Course design, quality matters training, and student outcomes. *American Journal of Distance Education,* 31(3), 207-216.

[25] Yusuf, N., & Al-Banawi, N. (2013). The impact of changing technology: The case of e-learning. *Contemporary Issues in Education Research (CIER)*, 6(2), 173-180.

[26] Morris, D. (2008). Economies of scale and scope in e-learning. *Studies in higher education*, 33(3), 331-343.

[27] Rodgers, T. (2008). Student engagement in the e-learning process and the impact on their grades. *International Journal of Cyber Society and Education,* 1(2), 143-156.

[28] Angelo, T. A., & Cross, P. (1993) *Classroom Assessment Techniques: A Handbook for College Teachers*. San Francisco: Jossey-Bass.

[29] Fink, L. D. (2003) *Creating Significant Learning Experiences: An Integrated Approach to Designing College Courses*. San Francisco: Jossey-Bass.

[30] Suskie, L. (2004) *Assessing Student Learning: A Common Sense Guide*. Bolton MA: Anker Publishing Company, Inc.

[31] Walvoord, B. E. (2004) *Assessment Clear and Simple: A Practical Guide for Institutions, Departments, and General Education*. San Francisco: Jossey-Bass.

Chapter 9

Emerging Technologies in Finance and Market: Applications of AI

Arshi Naim*
Department of Information Systems, King Khalid University,
Abha, Kingdom of Saudi Arabia (KSA)

Abstract

This is an extended chapter based on qualitative methods for the benefits of Artificial Intelligence (AI) which is the most growing branch of computer science and most of the service sectors are obtaining benefits from its application. This chapter provides a general role of AI in financial services and its definition in practical scenarios. The study is mostly qualitative and does not include any data analysis for its results. This article describes the major benefits derived by the practices of AI in general in the banking and financing firms. For the study, some examples of the role of AI in financial firms are analyzed and results are given from the positive observation shared by the FI firms on their official website. Since the data are available publically, the chapter did not find issues of data privacy and gave all references of data sources. AI benefits both service providers and users; this research report explains the advantages of AI in finance and also describes how AI can aid in market development. This chapter contributes positively in understanding the relevance of AI particularly in the field of finance.

* Corresponding Author's Email: arshi@kku.edu.sa.

In: Competitive Trends and Technologies in Business Management
Editors: Arshi Naim and Praveen K. Malik
ISBN: 978-1-68507-612-2

Keywords: artificial intelligence, financial services, financial stability, market development

1. Introduction

Artificial intelligence (AI) has been accepted for various applications and benefits by industries for Financial Services (FS). Therefore it is imperative to examine the role and advantages of AI in a financial context such as how AI helps in achieving Financial Stabilities (FSt). The use of AI in FS is growing very significantly and incredibly.

The range of AI's implication is varied like AI works for supply and demand factors in FS. The supply factors include advancements in technology, and for demand, it explains opportunities for profitability and level of competition. There are many applications of AI applied in present financial services that include [2], Financial Institutions (FI), vendors to automate client's interaction, measure credit quality concerning prices and in context to market insurance contracts. FI can identify scarce resources and analyze the influence of the market value of the firm with the help of AI. AI facilitates FI and other firms to evaluate Return on Investment (ROI) and establish the correlation between funds available, allocation of resources, and hedging of the funds. It is not always beneficial to adopting any technology because both advantages and disadvantages are associated with using it. AI has also given rise to some issues about handling and privacy of data. Some problems have arisen due to AI applications [1] such as the question of efficiency in the processing of information, how certain decisions may lead to achieving stability in the financial system, etc. These decisions may include decisions for credit, Financial Markets (FM), insurance contracts, and interactions with customers [4]. Another issue is about more dependencies on emerging technologies for achieving FSt [4]. Last but not the least; AI considers many irrelevant and not related factors for achieving and measuring FSt [4]. This research article includes an exemplary scenario of the role of AI in PricewaterhouseCoopers (PWC), India.

Machine learning (ML) is a subset of artificial intelligence (AI) that utilizes algorithms and computer power to sharpen the judgments organizations make about voluminous and disparate data. ML allows machines to learn how to perform certain tasks without being explicitly programmed to do so and PWC follows this philosophy in managing its financial services [13].

Despite the incredible progress and promise made possible by advances in financial artificial intelligence, it nevertheless presents some serious, interconnected risks and limitations. There are four categories of risks and limitations such as programming codes, data bias, virtual threats, and systemic risks. Artificial Intelligence is an indispensable part of the finance world due to its ability to understand complex mathematical relationships and its automation ability. With data and compute power growing exponentially, financial service providers are turning to AI for cost-effective solutions.

2. Literature Review

AI and ML are fast-paced growing technologies and have been adopted by diverse fields [2]. This research deals with the role of AI in FS.

Father of AI John McCarthy defined AI as the science of making intelligent machines, especially intelligent computer programs [2, 7, 9].

AI began its journey in the 1950s with the Dartmouth Summer Research Project on AI at Dartmouth College, USA [4]. There are not many firms working without the use of AI in recent years because AI systems deliver more creative services and results oriented [1, 4].

PricewaterhouseCoopers (PWC) is a UK based second-largest service providing professional organization in the world. It is operating in many countries and India is one of them [9]. This firm has partners across the globe and it is a lead firm in AI technologies, Data and Analytics [7-9]. PWC India has been applying AI in broader financial decisions to individual decisions. PWC India elucidates an application of AI techniques at clients as well as the firm's level [9].

The field of AI research was founded at a workshop held on the campus of Dartmouth College during the summer of 1956 [7]. Those who attended would become the leaders of AI research for decades. Many of them predicted that a machine as intelligent as a human being would exist in no more than a generation, and they were given millions of dollars to make this vision come true [8]. Eventually, it became obvious that commercial developers and researchers had grossly underestimated the difficulty of the project [8]. In 1973, in response to the criticism from James Lighthill and ongoing pressure from congress, the U. S. and British Governments stopped funding undirected research into AI, and the difficult years that followed would later be known as an "AI winter." Seven years later, a visionary initiative by the Japanese Government inspired governments and industry to provide AI with billions of dollars, but by the late 80s the investors became disillusioned and withdrew funding again [9].

Investment and interest in AI boomed in the first decades of the 21st century when ML was successfully applied to many problems in academia and industry due to new methods, the application of powerful computer hardware, and the collection of immense data sets.

Experts were welcoming of the innovative technology, and AI flourished until the 1970s.

The 1980s was the time when AI began to gain prominence in the finance world. This was when Expert systems emerged as an excellent commercial product in the field of finance. Until the 1980s, the Expert System (intelligence system based on knowledge) was used in the financial industry to predict market trends and provide customized financial plans [10].

The banking industry and financial institutions began to increasingly use expert systems to reduce the risks of human mistakes. It helped in financial analysis, market analysis, business development, international business, currency exchange, or bank management. Edward Feigenbaum introduced expert systems in 1980, which emulated the decision-making expertise of a human [10].

Dupont built 100 expert systems which helped them save nearly $10 million a year. The Protrader expert system designed by KC. Chen and Ting-peng Lian were among the first expert systems that forewarned the 87-point drop in DJIA in 1986.

At the same time, Applied Expert Systems (APEX), called the PlanPowerOne, was the first expert system that helped with financial plans. It was first commercially shipped in 1986, and it helped create financial plans for people with annual income over $75,000. Similarly, a Client Profiling System designed financial goals in the range of $25,000 and $200,000 a year [10]. In 2003, Hodgkinson and Walker developed a rule-based Expert System to help financial intuitions make underwriting decisions on credit application of corporate loans.

In 2009, LY Shue, CW Chen, W Shiue established an Expert System that contains the domain and operational knowledge base to conduct ontology-based ranking of listed companies in the Taiwan stock market [10].

Janulevicius and Goranin, in 2013, built up a risk management Expert System to enable medium and small-sized enterprises to conduct professional data security analysis due to capital constraints [11].

AI has been adopted more by service industries such as FIs and hospitals, etc. in developing markets. Service industries have started applying AI systems for several benefits such as fraud detection, diagnosis of diseases, illustrating and identifying side effects, detecting prognosis, etc. [8-10].

3. Discussion

In the current scenario sharing and analyzing of information has taken a digital platform and AI has a critical role in its working. For instance, AI specifically uses algorithms to automate the processing of financial data for market development [3]. AI develops a liaison between FS markets; resolves issues pertaining to buying and selling and enhances decision-making processes. AI is an example of emerging technologies and FIs are extensively applying it in checking the financial data sets for developing infrastructure, creating reliable policies for market growth and financial trading.

A market development strategy [16] is defined as a product or service based long term policies to create needs in the businesses. Market development Strategy seeks AI's applications in achieving this objective. AI helps not only locally but marketing at the global level [17]. The empirical application of AI can be witnessed in financial market development. Some examples are in the exportation of licenses for different financial marketing firms, merging and assembling joint ventures, or direct investments at diversified levels. But the process of applying is not very simple because the financial market is inclusive of several crucial dependents and independent variables in the economic system [17]. Nation's economy is based on the financial market which concludes that surpluses and deficits have to be examined under many financial consequences. Tools and techniques of AI have tried to solve and support the process. The figure below explains more about the working part of the procedure. AI has also assisted financial markets in meeting their objectives such as augmenting the capability of the financial market to act efficiently as an intermediary, negotiator, and creation of needs. Some more instances of AI in facilitating financial markets on the supply side are to provide and allocate a wide range of financial instruments, offering choices of issuers, credit risks, etc. and the similar scenario at the demand side also where AI helps in making investment decisions to meet trends and demand levels eventually reducing the risk factors [17, 18]. There are highly liquid financial markets have the ability to accommodate large and varied issuance of financial instruments with minimum price effect which can be swiftly transformed and exchanged at a reasonable cost by the support of AI's application in automating the timeline and adding values also AI help

Financial institutions and banking sectors to lower the transaction cost, enhance the efficiency of routine operations and can predict reasonable interests targets [16-18].

FI uses AI's applications for three major benefits at the demand level such as identifying the opportunities for cost reduction, managing risk, and increase in productivity. Table 1 below shows the level at which AI aids in FI.

Every firm or FI clearly describes the reasons for using AI. For market development (MD), these techniques are used to reduce costs, manage risk, and increase productivity. Also, AI is used for enhancing decisions for developing new products, identifying the best services for clients, and developing effective connections between systems and staff [4, 5].

For example, the firm, PWC, India has listed in its study that it uses cases of AI for enhancing financial security systems [7-9]. The study also explains the methods through which AI systems benefit in FS by reducing human errors, automating the process, and contributing to financial analytics in decision-making processes [7-9].

Table 1. AI at Demand Level

Artificial Intelligence		
↓		
Financial Institutions		
↓		
Opportunities for cost reduction	Risk Management Gain	Productivity Improvement

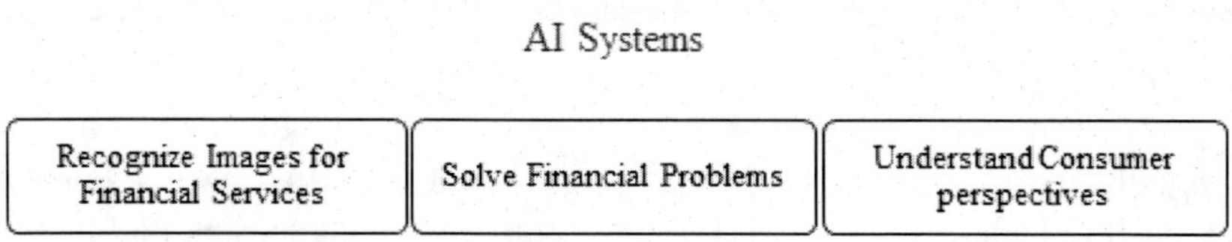

Figure 1. Working Model of AI in PWC, India [8].

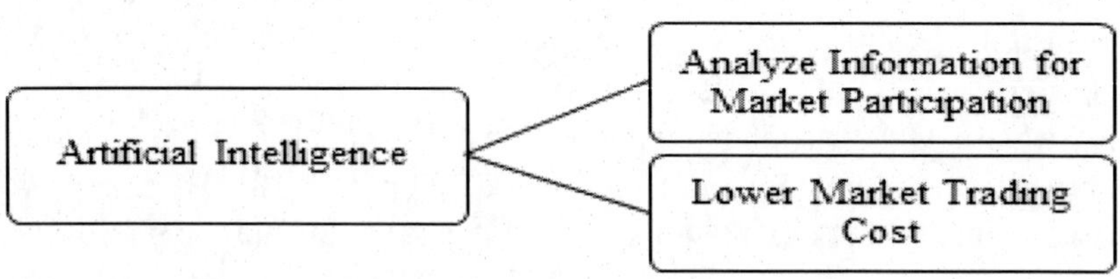

Figure 2. AI in Financial Market.

3.1. Micro Financial Point

FSt is dealt with at the micro-level and AI makes possible in describing the factors that need to be considered for financial stability and in recognizing the areas of improvements. Financial markets, consumers, and institutions are the players at a micro-level. Therefore it is vital to know how AI influences these parts. PWC, India annually prepares a report based on its financial results, consumers' survey, and stakeholder's satisfaction after using tools of AI in its working. PWC, India evidently concludes the importance of AI at its micro-level in financial perspectives.

3.2. Possible Effects of AI in Financial Markets

AI has the prospects to affect at the macro and micro level in FM. It can process financial information accurately, reduce all information distortion, and make the financial system more efficient. Therefore financial markets depending on AI for processing of information achieve better results than without using. PWC, India applies AI for analyzing information for market participants and for lowering market trading costs. Noticeably, AI affects service industries both at the micro and macro level.

AI techniques include the following in financial markets:

- AI uses several techniques in increasing financial market stabilities and development, like sentimental analysis to build up relationships with all key entities in FM, reduces all price irregularities, and develops effective pricing strategies. AI also assists in analyzing the information as a whole for the firm covering all major areas including financial decisions. For example PWC, India shows the role of AI in HRM, Financial decisions, Accounting decisions, user groups, etc. [9]

Most important reason for financial services to adopt AI is to lower market participants' trading costs that can comply with trading and investment strategies and develop markets for their consumers. AI also helps in discovering and reducing the prices over transaction costs.

The Financial Firm explains that AI can be used for credit scoring in FM. AI is used by financial sectors to explore opportunities and growth in businesses [8, 10, 12]. There are some businesses also that are capitalized by

AI in receiving benefits to produce quality data, accurate data, and cost efficiency [7-9]. These benefits clearly encourage FIs to apply AI in its work to achieve financial stability and developing markets.

3.3. Possible Effects of AI Learning on FI

It is assumed that if a firm is having large profitability consequently it will achieve financial stability. AI applications contribute to earning a good return on investment by controlling costs and monitoring other risk factors that prevent market growth.

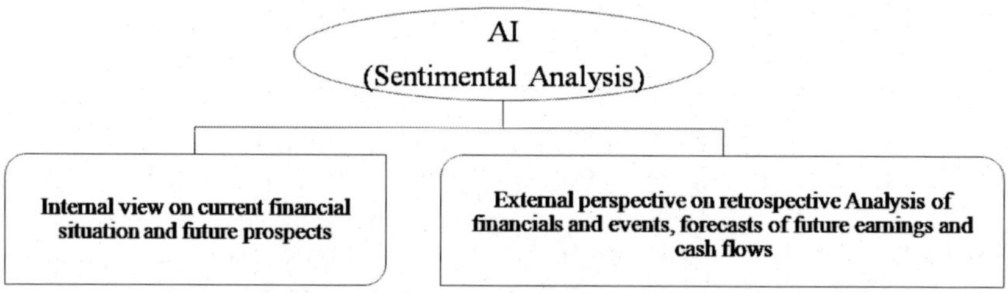

Figure 3. AI in PWC, India [9].

The firm explains that AI applications automate the business processes that result in reducing routine costs. Also, the FI can use AI to know their customers, how to achieve customer satisfaction, resource allocation, and new product development. In the current scenario, AI techniques are more used by FI for detecting fraud, identifying suspicious transactions, and cyber attacks. AI applications are used by FI for risk management too. This process is based on retrospective behavior of cash flows, various relations among prices of fixed assets, and revenue flow.

The firm describes that if financial decisions are mechanical by AI, it will offer accurate outcomes. Finance functions also indicate that AI is very impactful [10, 12] at all levels of operations.

3.4. Possible Effects of AI on Consumers and Investors

If AI reduces the costs and enhances the efficiency of FS, consumers can obtain several benefits.

AI aids customers in reducing borrowing costs increases the scope of financial services in their real life and can receive services and benefits based on their personal requirements. Another scope of AI is in big data analytics that can analyze the characteristics of customers that are available in the public domain. FI can take benefit of this analysis in understanding the consumer's needs and investors' requirements and accordingly can suggest financial products and services for them.

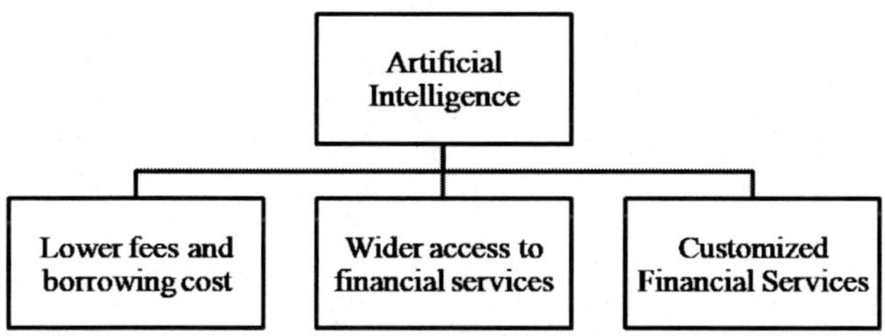

Figure 4. Role of AI on Consumers and investors.

Table 2. Impact of AI in the Financial System

Artificial Intelligence		
Financial Institutions		
Opportunities for cost reduction	Risk Management Gain	Productivity Improvement

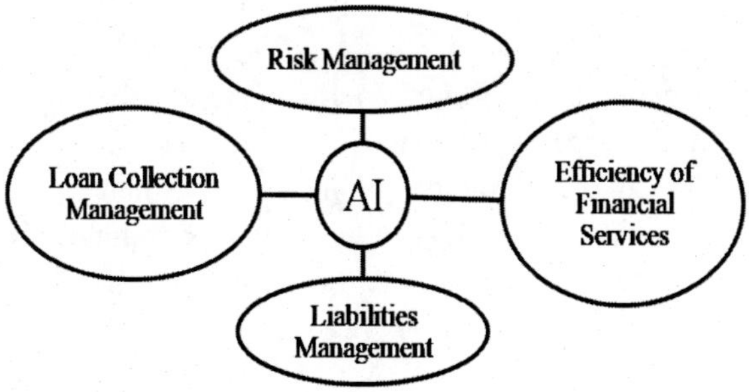

Figure 5. Benefits of AI in Finance Systems.

3.5. Macro-Financial Analysis

The application of AI to FS has capabilities to escalate the proficiency of the economy and contribute to understanding the need for adoption of AI that can affect the financial systems on the whole [2, 7].

Table 2 gives a clear picture that AI contributes in three imperative areas in financial systems namely, IEFS, DAES, and SIAI.

Table 3. AI Potentials in PWC, India [9]

Areas valued by AI	AI Potentials
AI stimulating Economic growth	Financial services using AI powered solutions like digital assistant, recommender systems, etc for helping financial clients and financial businesses for sharing data freely. Along with enhancing financial security systems.
AI as Customer care	Some systems of AI like chatbots, digital assistants and robots can conduct and help financial clients, offer solutions to financial issues, give information on new financial products and services.
AI for market growth	AI applications can integrate business processes, reduce costs, and bring higher productivity, growth and efficiency.

AI has contributed to providing benefits to clients; they can make effective financial decisions, allocate funds, and utilize them optimally. AI has made it possible to diminish the costs of payments for financial clients. AI has provided achievable standards for FIs by satisfying financial consumers with FS, by managing risk, liabilities, and loan portfolio. AI also elaborates the economies of scope for FI while realizing the relationship with other institutions in service sectors.

This film explores how AI creates opportunities for financial and non-financial firms to grow together and get involved in research and development to stimulate economic growth. Macro financial aspects provide a range of benefits for the adoption of AI. It can be implemented from short term to long term economic growth.

This organization expresses the potentialities of AI in FS. AI focuses on financial systems from several perspectives, like how to stimulate economic growth so that FS using AI-powered solutions can provide relevant financial data and security systems. AI assists financial clients by informing new financial products, investment decisions, and solving financial problems. AI presents solutions to high costs and the lack of technical expertise. AI applications can integrate business processes, reduce costs, and bring higher productivity, growth, and efficiency.

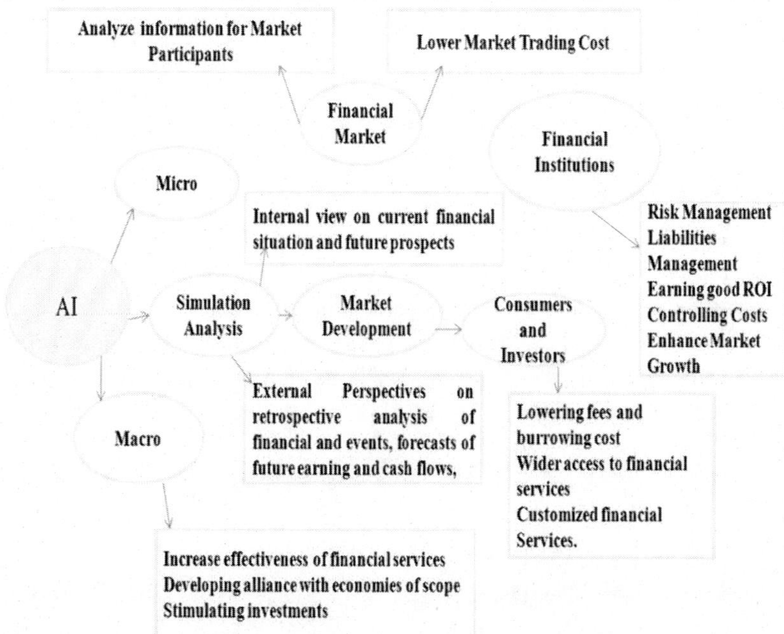

Figure 6. Role of AI in FS.

4. Results

This chapter has concluded that AI provides key benefits to all service industries. There are many applications of AI used invariably by these service industries but this descriptive study explains the relevance and applications in Financial Systems and in developing the market in general.

The above given table presents the comprehensive environment of AI application in FS. AI has been adopted to achieve benefits at various levels of micro and macro. This research article has illustrated the significance of AI and how it impetuses and exhibits the growth of the service industry in general and specifically for the financial sector. Since this paper deals with financial sectors we tried to identify the key benefits provided by AI for financial institutions and financial customers. Through the example of PWC, we presented the concern and benefits of AI in FS and for market development too.

The discussion part clearly explained how AI is playing a great role in PWC as an example and for any financial service providers in developing markets, achieving customers' satisfaction, enhancing security systems, controlling costs, managing risk factors, etc.

Conclusion

The use of AI will continue to be used more and more by service sectors and its various applications will make the services more autonomous, accurate, and cost-effective. Customer satisfaction and trust will be achieved by the service providers by using AI in their working and they will be able to provide more customized features too. Also, AI will play a more vital role in enhancing security systems, especially in the financial sectors.

References

[1] Advantages and Disadvantages, issues of allocation of AI in *FS "European Joint Committee Discussion Paper on the Use of AI by FI,"* Jonathan Stuart Ward and Adam Barker (2016).

[2] "Definition of AI," Arthur Samuel (1959), for AI. *IBM Journal*: 211-229; Tom Mitchell (1997), AI and Machine Learning, New York: McGraw Hill; Michael Jordan and Tom Mitchell (2015) "Trends, perspectives, and prospects," *Science* 349(6245): 255-26.

[3] AI in algorithm, Thomas Cover and Peter Hart (1967), "Nearest Neighbor Pattern Classification," *IEEE transactions on information theory*. 13.1: 21-27. See Luke Dormehl (2016), Thinking Machines: The Quest for Artificial Intelligence-and Where It's Taking Us Next, London: Penguin Books.

[4] Naim, A. (2021). Application of Quality Matters in Digital Learning in Higher Education. *Texas Journal of Multidisciplinary Studies*, 1(1), 3-12.

[5] Dependencies in Emerging technologies, Tim Dettmers (2015), "History of AI," *Parallel Forall,* December 2017 (Available on https://devblogs.nvidia.com/parallelforall/deep-learning-nutshell-history-training/).

[6] "AI in Assessing Risks: a Regulatory Perspective," *OpRisk North America*, June 21. Bauguess (2017). Gerard Hoberg and Craig M. Lewis (2015).

[7] AI in FS and for FSt Brynjolfsson, E. & McAfee, A. (2017). The business of artificial intelligence. *Harvard Business Review* (Available on from https://hbr.org/coverstory/).

[8] *Importance of AI in services PwC. India* (2017) (Available on http://www.pwc.com/gx/en/issues/analytics/assets/pwc-ai-analysis-sizing-017/07/the-business-of-artificial-intelligence).

[9] Hussain, M. R., Quadri, N. N., Ahmad, N., Qamar, S., Khan, N., Naim, A., & Hussain, M. E. (2019, April). Effective cost optimization approach in Healthcare to Minimize the treatment cost of Brain-tumor Patients. In: *2019 International Conference on Computer and Information Sciences (ICCIS)* (pp. 1-5). IEEE.

[10] Policies of AI (2017), *AI technology implications, PWC, India Research Papers* (Available on http://www.nedo.go.jp/content/ 100865202.pdf).

[11] AI used by Financial sectors, "explore opportinies, provide correct and reliable data" "achieve cost effectiveness by AI" Application of AI Bauguess (2017).

[12] *AI in business, "effectiveness" "market development,"* Rao, A. (2017) (Available on https://www.strategy-business.com/article/A-Strategists-Guide-to-ArtificialIntelligence).

[13] *Changes in service industries with the application of AI, PwC.* (2017) (Available on https://www.pwc.com/us/en/industry/entertainment-media/publications/consumer-intelligence-series/ assets/pwc-botme).

[14] *Market Development, achieving ROI, appropriate application of AI, results from the Survey PwC,* India (2017) (Available on http://www.pwc.in/assets/pdfs/publications/ceo-survey/20th-ceosurvey-being-fit-for-growth.pdfoklet.pdf).

[15] *New era of AI and machine learning*. Knight W. (2017) (Available on https://www.technologyreview.com/s/609038/chinas-ai).

[16] *An decade of electronics, moving with AI in services PwC*. (2017), India (Available on https://www.pwc.com/us/en/advisory-services/ digital-iq/assets/pwc-digital-iq-report.pdf-awakening/).

[17] AI for present scenario in FS and future of AI in service industries, Sara El-Hanfy (Posted on: 13 June 2018 - Categories): I, *Industrial strategy*

challenge fund AI, Next Generation Services (Available on https://innovateuk.blog.gov.uk/).

[18] Kumar V, Rajan B, Venkatesan R, Lecinski J. Understanding the Role of Artificial Intelligence in Personalized Engagement Marketing. *Sage publications California Management Review*. 2019;61(4):135-155. doi:10.1177/0008125619859317.

[19] Popkova E. G., Parakhina V. N. (2019) Managing the Global Financial System on the Basis of Artificial Intelligence: Possibilities and Limitations. In: Popkova E. (eds.) The Future of the Global Financial System: Downfall or Harmony. ISC 2018. *Lecture Notes in Networks and Systems*, vol 57. Springer, Cham. https://doi.org/ 10.1007/978-3-030-00102-5_100.

[20] Ahmadi, M., Jafarzadeh-Ghoushchi, S., Taghizadeh, R. et al. Presentation of a new hybrid approach for forecasting economic growth using artificial intelligence approaches. *Neural Computer & Application* 31, 8661-8680 (2019) Springer. https://doi.org/10.1007/ s00521-019-04417-0.

[21] Khan, N., Naim, A., Hussain, M. R., Naveed, Q. N., Ahmad, N., & Qamar, S. (2019, May). The 51 v's of big data: survey, technologies, characteristics, opportunities, issues and challenges. In: *Proceedings of the international conference on omni-layer intelligent systems* (pp. 19-24).

[22] Naim, A., & Alahmari, F. (2020). Reference model of e-learning and quality to establish interoperability in higher education systems. *International Journal of Emerging Technologies in Learning (iJET),* 15(2), 15-28.

[23] Naim, A., Khan, M. F., Hussain, M. R., & Khan, N. (2019). "Virtual Doctor" Management Technique in the Diagnosis of ENT Diseases. *JOE*, 15(9), 88.

[24] Naim, A., Alahmari, F., & Rahim, A. (2021). Role of Artificial Intelligence in Market Development and Vehicular Communication. *Smart Antennas: Recent Trends in Design and Applications*, 2, 28.

[25] Naim, A. (2020). Realization of diverse Electronic tools in learning and teaching for students with diverse skills. *Global Journal of Enterprise Information System*, 12(1), 72-78.

[26] Naim, A., & Bashir, A. (2016). Application of Quality Matters Standards on Supportive and Online Module in Higher Education Program. *Research Revolution*, 5(3), 6-12.

About the Editors

Dr. Arshi Naim

Department of Information Systems,
King Khalid University, AlSAmer,
King Khalid University, Abha, Kingdom of Saudi Arabia (KSA)

Dr. Arshi Naim is working in Department of Information Systems, College of Computer Science, King Khalid University, which is an NCAAA accredited University. He is a pioneer member who was introduced to the concept of Quality and Accreditation process in the University and is currently a member of Academic Development and Quality Committee. He is contributing in preparing a self-study report for the program, evaluating course documents and other Accreditation related documents. He has developed Business Information Systems modules, like E-Commerce, Accounting Information systems, Information Systems Strategic management, Marketing Strategies, etc. and has expertise in writing course specifications, course reports and course learning outcomes. He has been working on developing study plans and curricula for undergraduates and postgraduate programs. He also contributes as an E-learning expert and has received many excellence awards in developing online courses from Quality Matters US. He is also a peer reviewer for online courses from KKU E-Learning Deanship. He has received an International Academic Award from QM for the course E-Commerce conducted by King Khalid University and Certificate of Appreciation for successful online Instructor for conducting blended courses from 2014 to 2016 in E-learning. He is currently instructing Business Information related modules in full online platform and face to face.

Email: arshi@kku.edu.sa; arshi_naim@rediffmail.com
Orcid: https://orcid.org/0000-0003-1325-6964
LinkedIn: https://www.linkedin.com/in/arshi-naim-503ba7131/
Google Scholar:
https://scholar.google.com/citations?hl=en&user=UayrGdcAAAAJ
Scopus id: https://www.scopus.com/authid/detail.uri?authorId=57209199862

Dr. Praveen K. Malik
School of Electronics and Electrical Engineering,
Lovely Professional University, Phagwara, Punjab, India

Dr. Praveen K. Malik is a Professor in the School of Electronics and Electrical Engineering, Lovely Professional University, Phagwara, Punjab, India. His current research interests include Microstrip Antenna Design, MIMO, Vehicular Communication and IoT. He has published three edited/authored academic books. He is Associate Editor of several Journals including *International Journal of Science and Engineering Research*, *Asian Journal of Management, Engineering and Computer Science*, *International Journal of Engineering Research & Technology (IJERT)* and *International Journal of Antennas*. He has filed two patents successfully. He holds a PhD with a specialization in Wireless Communication and Antenna Design.

Email: pkmalikmeerut@gmail.com; praveen.23314@lpu.co.in
Orcid: https://orcid.org/0000-0003-3433-8248
Researchgate: https://www.researchgate.net/profile/Praveen_Malik5
LinkedIn: https://www.linkedin.com/in/praveen-malik-b664b412a
Scopus id: https://www.scopus.com/authid/detail.uri?authorId=55137130500
https://www.mendeley.com/authors/55137130500/
Twitter: https://twitter.com/PraveenMalik24

Index

A

B

C

D

E

F

T

W